BUILD THE FORT

CHRIS HEIVLY

FOREWORD BY BRAD FELD

BUILD | THE | FORT

THE STARTUP COMMUNITY
BUILDER'S FIELD GUIDE

BUILD THE FORT PUBLISHING

BUILD THE FORT
The Startup Community Builder's Field Guide

FIRST EDITION

ISBN 978-1-5445-4259-1 *Hardcover*
      978-1-5445-4260-7 *Paperback*
      978-1-5445-4261-4 *Ebook*

For Patty, who smiles at every one of my crazy ideas.

CONTENTS

FOREWORD 13

PREFACE 17

INTRODUCTION 21

FOUNDATION: THE BASIC BUILDING BLOCKS AND PRINCIPLES OF A STARTUP COMMUNITY

1. COMMUNITY TRUTHS 31

STARTUP COMMUNITIES ARE COMPLEX SYSTEMS 32

STARTUP COMMUNITY BUILDING IS FOR EVERYONE!
(IS THIS YOU?) 39

SO, YOU'RE A COMMUNITY BUILDER? 42

ARE YOU READY TO PLAY AN IMPACTFUL ROLE IN YOUR
COMMUNITY? 45

2. BUILDING PRINCIPLES 47

PRINCIPLE #1: IDENTIFY ALL ACTORS 48

PRINCIPLE #2: PARTNER 51

PRINCIPLE #3: ASSESS AND LEVERAGE ASSETS 55

PRINCIPLE #4: APPLY A SHORT-TERM MINDSET 60

PRINCIPLE #5: BUILD THE FORT 69

FRAMEWORK: THE COMPONENTS OF
STARTUP COMMUNITY BUILDING

THREE FRAMEWORKS 75

3. **ASSET FRAMEWORK** **77**
   ACTORS 78
   ACTIVITIES 80
   ATTITUDES... 83

4. **ECOSYSTEM MATURITY FRAMEWORK** **89**
   STAGES OF ECOSYSTEM MATURITY....................... 90
      Nascent Stage 91
      Developing Stage 93
      Emerging Stage 94
      Leading Stage.................................... 95

5. **ENGAGEMENT FRAMEWORK** **99**
   DRIVER #1: DEVELOP LEADERS............................ 100
      The Pledge..................................... 103
      An Influencer Circle 103
      Amplify Your Voice 106
      Open Office Hours............................. 107
      Local Coffees, Meetups, Panels, Conferences 107
      Blogs, Twitter, Facebook, and Instagram.............110
   DRIVER #2: DEVELOP FOUNDERS 111
      Idea Programs and Seminars.................115
      Open Office Hours............................116
      Startup Weekend 117
      Pitch Competition 117
      Coffee Meetups 118
      Beer Meetup...................................118
      Hackathon 119

DRIVER #3: DEVELOP MENTORS 119

    Accelerator.....................121

    Workshops.....................122

    Open Office Hours.....................123

    Peer Dinners 125

    The Non-Local Network Connection 125

    What Makes a Good Mentor? 126

    The Mentor Manifesto 127

DRIVER #4: DEVELOP INVESTORS 130

    Angel Awareness 132

    Deal Flow 133

    Angel Dinners 134

    Angel Group.....................135

    Outside Investors 136

DRIVER #5: ENGAGE CORPORATIONS 138

    Why Should Local Corporations Care? 139

    The Corporate Mentor 141

    Alpha | Beta | First Customer 142

    Sponsorship 143

    The Corporation as Funder.....................143

    Mergers and Acquisitions.....................144

DRIVER #6: ENGAGE UNIVERSITIES.....................145

    How to Teach Entrepreneurship 146

    Guest Speaking.....................147

    Community, Meet Students 148

    Curriculum 149

    Tech Transfer/University IP.....................149

    Pitch Event 151

    Alumni Fund.....................152

DRIVER #7: ENGAGE GOVERNMENT.....................153

    Customer 155

    Host Event.....................156

Sponsorship 156

Funder 157

Policy.. 161

    Business Formation 161

    Business Termination...................................... 162

    Tax Policy... 163

    A Policy Strategy 164

ACTION: THE FINAL TOUCHES ON THE ECOSYSTEM BUILD

6. ECOSYSTEM GAME PLAN 167

STEP ONE: COMMUNITY AUDIT 168

STEP TWO: COMMUNITY OR ECOSYSTEM?........................... 170

STEP THREE: APPLY THE THREE FRAMEWORKS TO YOUR
ECOSYSTEM GAME PLAN 173

    Nascent Stage 174

        Priorities 174

        Risks 175

    Developing Stage 176

        Priorities 176

        Risks 178

    Emerging Stage 179

        Priorities 179

        Risks 182

    Leading Stage.. 184

        Priorities 184

        Risks 185

7. WE GOTTA MEASURE, DON'T WE? 187

WHY WE MEASURE... 188

THE TYPICAL USELESS MEASUREMENT DATA......................... 189

    Capital.. 190

Jobs 192

MEASURE WHAT MATTERS 193

    The Network 195

    Founder Sentiment 197

    Community Behaviors 198

CONCLUSION **201**

APPENDIX **203**

DEFINITIONS (YES, IT'S THAT IMPORTANT) 203

CONCEPTS 203

ORGANIZATIONS 205

PEOPLE 206

MY STARTUP COMMUNITY THOUGHT LEADERS/

ORGANIZATIONS 207

FURTHER READING (BOOKS THAT INSPIRED ME) 207

ACKNOWLEDGMENTS **209**

ABOUT THE AUTHOR **211**

YOUR STARTUP COMMUNITY **215**

FOREWORD

—BRAD FELD
BOULDER, COLORADO
NOVEMBER 2022

After selling my first, Boston-based company in 1993, my wife, Amy Batchelor, and I decided to move to Boulder, Colorado. It was a random, lifestyle-based decision. We only knew one person living there and had only been there once for a few days on vacation, but we occasionally watched a *Mork and Mindy* episode.

Upon arriving in Boulder, I discovered that it was an intelligent community with many PhDs because of the University of Colorado and several government labs. In addition, there was a long history of technology companies in the area, although cable, telecom, and the storage industry dominated the success stories. But I also heard that Boulder needed more management talent, especially for software companies.

Over twenty-five years later, Boulder is one of the best cities in the world to create and scale a high-growth business. It also continues to be a magnificent place to live. While the startup community has many strengths, it also has weaknesses, reinforcing that building a startup community is never finished.

As Boulder's startup community became famous, people often asked me the secret. I said, "Don't try to be Silicon Valley. Instead, build on your city's unique strengths." By 2012, I had four principles, which I called the Boulder Thesis.

1. Entrepreneurs must lead the startup community.
2. The leaders must have a long-term commitment.
3. The startup community must be inclusive of anyone who wants to participate in it.
4. The startup community must have continual activities that engage the entire entrepreneurial stack.

At the time, much of the Boulder Thesis was controversial, especially among many people who thought the solution was to either be like Silicon Valley or simply attract more capital, especially venture capital, to the city.

Today, the Boulder Thesis is at the core of startup community activity worldwide. As entrepreneurship became democratized globally, I continued to learn how startup communities worked and what helped or hindered them. Finally, I concluded—and began asserting—that any city with at least 100,000 people (the size of Boulder) needed a vibrant startup community to help it stay healthy and innovative over a long time.

In 2020, I came out with a new book with Ian Hathaway called *The Startup Community Way*, inspired by Eric Ries's book *The Startup Way*. One of the insights Ian and I had, which we built the book around, was that startup communities are complex adaptive systems. They are unpredictable. As they develop, they are unique. They evolve based on what has recently happened. As a result, no playbooks, rules, recipes, or plans are generically applicable. Instead, there are frameworks, principles, and roles for people and organizations to rally around.

One of the critical elements of a complex system is a bottom-up, network-driven, peer approach versus a top-down, hierarchical, patriarchal approach. When people try to control or engineer a complex system, it fails. Instead of focusing on the parts, you need to work on the interaction between the parts.

Once you understand this, the logical question is, "Great, Brad. But what do I do next?" While Ian and I covered some ideas in *The Startup Community Way*, Chris took it to the next level with this book.

I met Chris a dozen years ago when he wanted to learn from my experience in Boulder as he began to help build the startup community in Raleigh-Durham, North Carolina. After that, we stayed connected, especially around The Startup Factory (his accelerator), Techstars, and several initiatives.

Chris visited me in Boulder in late 2016. He was thinking about helping the fifteen-plus cities within a four-hour drive from his home in Durham build startup communities and evolve their entrepreneurial ecosystems. David Cohen, one of the Techstars co-founders, and I had discussed something similar for Techstars. So why not work on this together?

Chris, with Ian, led an effort at Techstars that advanced the idea of "startup communities as complex systems." As with any complex system, this was a continuous, iterative, and evolving effort with both successes and failures. But, each output generated new inputs, and Chris immersed himself in bridging theory with practice.

This book is about the practice. As part of this, Chris simplifies the complex (pun intended).

In Chris's first book, *Build the Fort: Why 5 Simple Lessons You Learned as a 10-Year-Old Can Set You Up for Startup Success*, Chris provided new founders with a fort-building framework that helps eliminate the adult noise in their brains and helps them to think more like ten-year-old fort builders.

In *Build the Fort: The Startup Community Builder's Field Guide*, Chris simplifies the complex by breaking down and providing actionable steps for implementing vital elements from *The Startup Community Way*.

When Chris first told me about his idea for this book, he envisioned it as a complement to *The Startup Community Way*. I strongly encouraged that and am delighted to see it come to life.

PREFACE

For as long as I can remember, I had this dream of buying an old building, gutting it, and setting it up for new tech founders. The idea would be to set up a server room, run CAT-5 to all the floors and offices, and invite in a few of my favorite experts (software developers, marketing folks, and generally people who like to get shit done).

And then I started reading about Techstars and Y Combinator—basically the quasi-virtual versions of my dream. First-time founders figuring out how to put their ideas into play. Experienced and motivated mentors engaging with the founders in meaningful ways. Energy. Sparks. Laughter. Encouragement. Fellowship. Count me in!

In the fall of 2009, both these groups had run two to three annual versions of their new-age incubator programs (now referred to as accelerators). The press was starting to write about the programs, the entrepreneurs, and their unique experiences.

I launched the Triangle Startup Factory in Raleigh-Durham,

North Carolina, in the fall of 2009. I ran my first accelerator program in fall of 2010 under the name Launchbox Digital, which later changed to The Startup Factory (TSF), until fall of 2016. When I started working on the concept in 2009, I was lucky enough to connect with David Cohen and Brad Feld (two of four Techstars co-founders). David shared what he knew about running a great accelerator program, and Brad offered what he was learning about how to build a robust community. We've maintained a great relationship ever since.

Why is this important? Because these vehicles opened the door for me to serve as a startup community builder for the past thirteen years in my adopted hometown. Through my work in Raleigh-Durham, I went on to create numerous founder-oriented activities that helped propel the region into one of the fastest-growing startup communities in the world.

I share this preface as a means to ground you in the truth that I've been where you are. I've been in important-person meetings and have rolled up my sleeves with community enthusiasts to push our ecosystem forward from the streets.

In 2012, Brad Feld wrote the first book I had ever seen on this topic, called *Startup Communities*. My partner in TSF, Dave Neal, and I devoured the book, deconstructed it, and built a game plan for our region based on its concepts. It was an important, even critical, inspiration for us as well as many others.

In his book, Brad shares various activities that they stood up in Boulder and how they fit into his meta-message, but I found that many community leaders just replicated the activities and missed the "collaborate and support others" thread that runs through the book. I know that this core mindset and behavior—collaboration and support—was instrumental in our success in Raleigh-Durham.

Fast-forward to late 2016, when Brad, David Cohen, and I sat in Boulder and started brainstorming how we could help other startup community enthusiasts. I was getting inbound requests from Charlotte, Greensboro, and Wilmington, North Carolina; Richmond and Norfolk, Virginia; and many other mid-tier cities. Techstars was getting the same requests, but from all over the world. What could we do to support them in a more methodical manner?

In our heart, we are all founders, and we take that perspective when addressing new opportunities. Our "Ecosystem Development" initiative, piloted in 2017 and launched formally in 2018, outlined two main challenges:

1. Identify an updated, high-level strategy that recognizes that one single game plan doesn't fit every city.
2. Create, test, and implement a set of tactics that can bend to each city's unique qualities.

Along the way, my friends and partners in the startup consulting business began to develop a new book. *The Startup Community Way*, authored by Brad Feld and Ian Hathaway, is obviously an important driver, but where it masters the strategy of effective ecosystem building, it stops short on tactics. This was on purpose, as we decided to split our thinking into two books in 2019.

As Brad shared in the foreword, this book is a complement to *The Startup Community Way*, and as such I will refer to various elements of it. Complex systems, and the science behind them as it relates to startup communities, are the smartest and most relevant frameworks I see today.

INTRODUCTION

There is not a day that goes by without a reference to Facebook, Amazon, Apple, Google, or any other high-tech/high-growth company finding a way into your life. Every city leader who cares about the economic impact of their region yearns to have these types of companies and their requisite jobs in their backyard. But the success of these businesses is no accident—they didn't grow to this size and impact in a vacuum. They're the products of incredible startup communities.

Today, city leaders from all over the world are striving to create the type of startup communities or entrepreneurial ecosystems that serve as part of their future economic development strategies. They've poured hundreds of millions of dollars and years of effort into duplicating the venerable Silicon Valley. But for the most part, those dollars and hours haven't come close to achieving the goals those leaders imagined for their cities.

I have been deeply involved in building startup communities in my adopted town of Raleigh-Durham, North Carolina, for over thirteen years now. More recently I built a consulting business centered on coaching, building, and accelerating startup communities and entrepreneurial ecosystems around the world. I've worked with entrepreneurs, business leaders, and policymakers in cities such as Louisville, Kentucky; Columbia, South Carolina; and Buffalo, New York; as well as across the globe in Peru, Taiwan, and Western Canada. During that time, I've learned what works and what doesn't based on each region's unique characteristics.

In late December 2016 I was between gigs again. My partner Dave Neal and I had ceased operations of our investment accelerator, The Startup Factory (TSF), after four and a half years and thirty-five investments. I had a few conversations with David Cohen, CEO of Techstars, about opening up a Techstars program to replace TSF, and he offered to host me for a day in Boulder to compare notes and connect with Brad Feld, David Brown, and Nicole Glaros, all important members of the Techstars executive team. Within days after that meeting, we decided to start a new business together focused on helping startup community builders establish and grow their entrepreneurial ecosystems.

Three weeks later we were ready to go!

From 2016 through 2021, I worked with Techstars leaders, as well as Cali Harris and Ian Hathaway and a bevy of smart, motivated Techstars staffers, in what we called "Ecosystem Development."

The good news is that our singular experiences in Boulder and Raleigh-Durham were augmented by our respective discussions with entrepreneurial leaders in quite a few cities around the world. In addition to those experiences, Brad, David, and Marc

Nagar had sat down a few months earlier and brainstormed an outline of how one might analyze the maturity of a given city or region. And, of course, we had Brad's seminal book on the topic published in 2012, *Startup Communities*, which my TSF partner, Dave Neal, and I deconstructed and used as a guide for our startup community–building activities in Raleigh-Durham.

Over the course of those five years, I led our team of twelve to build a tactical model for ecosystem development. I worked side by side with Cali Harris, my first partner in crime, and Ian Hathaway, who took the seeds of systems theory and expanded and molded them into ecosystem development. This collaboration also influenced Brad and Ian's recent book, *The Startup Community Way*.

Though these sources were valuable, there's nothing like getting your head beaten in by the market. "No business plan survives its first contact with a customer," said Steve Blank; ecosystem development was no exception to that edict. In the first year, we engaged in five three-month pilot projects in Richmond, Virginia; Okanagan, British Columbia, Canada; Fort Wayne, Indiana; Lima, Peru; and Cleveland, Ohio. I was a lone wolf conducting all of the interviews, testing and iterating on our model, and writing the final reports (as well as sharing those reports publicly). I needed to get my hands dirty and see this in action.

We followed up on the pilots with longer-term consulting engagements in Buffalo, New York; Taipei, Taiwan; Louisville, Kentucky; Norfolk, Virginia; and Knoxville, Tennessee. And we joined a handful of existing and future Techstars accelerator programs to better serve those regions by sprinkling in some ecosystem development.

These were the contracted engagements, but they pale in comparison to the connections we made and discussions we had with another fifty-plus cities and each of their community leaders.

If that background is the good news, I have to share the bad news.

There is no single playbook for building and accelerating your startup community that will work for every city.

However, there is a mindset and a process to move forward that can improve your chances of successfully growing your startup community. Think of this book as a field guide for motivated leaders like yourself.

Our tactical methodology is still a work in progress. Ian, Cali, Brad, and I still struggle with championing the complex mindset while at the same time trying to deliver and implement specific actions that have meaningful outcomes.

As adults we seem to make everything harder. Why is that? Why do we seem to add complexity, nuance, layers of emotion, and every piece of our psychology to even the most mundane of activities? Psychologists spend years trying to figure this out. Can't say I have an answer either. But I might have a solution.

In my first book, *Build the Fort: Why 5 Simple Lessons You Learned as a 10-Year-Old Can Set You Up for Startup Success*, I outlined a simple five-step methodology to help you release those adult demons.

Let me share my ten-year-old point of view.

I grew up in Newtown Square, Pennsylvania, which lies about twenty miles west of Philadelphia. When I was in that ten-to-fourteen-year-old age cohort, my friend Jimmy Doyle and I built forts. Lots of forts. Probably ten-plus as best I can remember. (Check out a wonderful fort-building story in my first book.) When I think back on that time and I break down our fort-building process from dream to reality, I'm surprised at the ease with which we accomplished our goals of building each one of those forts. Thinking about that spurred me to try to understand why it seemed so simple then, but why it seems so difficult today.

Take yourself back to when you were ten. Remember building a fort? Maybe it was outside with some wood you found. Maybe it was an inside fort and you turned your dining room chairs upside down, put them on the couch, and strung a blanket over them to form a tent. Maybe you added a broomstick in the middle to prop up the blanket. More importantly, do you remember how simple it was to build it without any adult angst?

The *Build the Fort* thesis is a simple metaphor with five actionable principles:

1. Share your ideas with others (what I now refer to as **Understanding Your Users**).
2. Find friends to help put your idea into action (develop your go-to **Team**).
3. Gather the things you need to move forward quickly (early-stage **Product Development**).
4. Set up small, short-term goals (finding the intersection of your **Long-Term Vision and Creating Small Wins** to build confidence and momentum).
5. Then do it! (Don't wait for **Permission or Perfect Data**.)

The purpose of this book is to give you a tool with which to combat that seemingly natural adult ability to complicate your goals. In *Build the Fort: The Startup Community Builder's Field Guide*, I will take you back to your ten-year-old self and help you use your perfect and pure brain to turn your community dreams and ideas into action.

My modus operandi has always been to simplify the complex in order to encourage specific actions so they don't seem as scary as we might imagine.

In that same manner, I want you to channel your ten-year-old self and think more like a child as you get motivated to build your startup community. For current and future community builders I lay out a simple framework of questions for effective ecosystem building:

1. What are a few simple truths to reorient your adult brain?
2. What factors motivate you to get involved in building your startup community?
3. How can the fort-building metaphor inspire and instruct you?
4. How does systems thinking provide a much-needed non-traditional mindset?
5. What are the core building blocks for startup community building?
6. What are the benchmarks for your community against the four stages of startup community maturity?
7. Have you developed and prioritized the seven drivers of startup community engagement?
8. Are you set up to measure progress?

Are you motivated to get involved in your local startup community? Are you curious and even concerned about what to focus on and how to be most impactful? Good, then this book is for you. Over the next few pages, I will blend our experiences in building and accelerating robust startup communities with a simple but actionable metaphor of fort building.

Thanks for flipping to the next page and enjoy the journey!

THE BASIC BUILDING BLOCKS AND PRINCIPLES OF A STARTUP COMMUNITY

On the surface, it seems so simple. Start a venture fund to invest in the best and brightest entrepreneurs in town and help them grow a great big company. Or build out a new innovation center where entrepreneurs can connect and access the resources they need. Or create a mentorship program assigning your local senior business executives (and people who you have worked with on many projects) to first-time founders to help them make better decisions. Or, find some business leaders who have built and scaled local companies and lean on their expertise, experience, and connections to drive all of these activities, and *bam!* we're in the game.

But are we playing the right game? And if not, what are the new building blocks and principles of *this* game?

CHAPTER 1

COMMUNITY TRUTHS

I've been a successful startup high-growth community builder for over thirteen years. Along the way, I captured eleven truths. Have fun with this chapter and think of these as a home base to come back to when you're trying to build consensus, raise money to support a new program, and engage with those who are disengaged.

1. Comparing communities is like comparing children—don't do it. Each community is unique and has relative strengths and weaknesses. The same techniques that work for one child/community do not work for another child/community.
2. Business leaders are generally consensus builders. Entrepreneurs bet against consensus. This personality conflict is why business leaders typically make for bad startup community builders.
3. Ill-informed leaders use a space (a building or physical location) as a leading indicator/influencing agent to measure the progress of a community. An innovation space is just one of many elements for a thriving or growing ecosystem.
4. The community leaders who are assigned the task of build-

ing a startup community (government, university, economic development, chamber, etc.) typically bring a "manager" mindset. This mindset almost always hinders progress.

5. There are two types of community builders: conveners (people who create meetups; organizers who find the space, schedule the time, and get people to an event), and influencers (the people others listen to). In many places, the convener thinks they are an influencer, but often they are not.

6. Marketing your community as a startup hub without its actually being a startup hub rarely works. It is an old-school economic development tactic that will turn off the best of your entrepreneurs.

7. Great community leaders support each other's efforts—it's not about hierarchy or super coordination. It is simply about supporting fellow passion projects.

8. Almost every active community leader inherently knows the available library of tactical activities—they just don't know the priorities and which set of activities to focus on when.

9. Community capacity is the notion that each community has a ceiling it can achieve for its community and its startups. A community builder's goal is to grow to that capacity and then increase it.

10. We measure the maturity of startup communities not to test against a standard or compare to others, but to reveal what a city's gaps are and where community builders' priorities lie.

11. Want to do something impactful right now? Spend more time connecting versus coordinating.

STARTUP COMMUNITIES ARE COMPLEX SYSTEMS

We all enjoy finding a model we can orient around, just as a map orients you to where you are and where you want to go. Startup communities are no different. We crave a model or set of rules, or at least a guideline of what works and what doesn't. Our fort-building metaphor works because it's a simple approach to getting our ideas out and launched. But remember, there is no map to building a great startup community—just a compass.

One area of science that seems to have promise is the application of systems theory. A system is a "cohesive conglomeration of interrelated and interdependent parts that are either natural or man-made."[1] Most of the research to date has been applied to biology, ecology, and psychology. Related subjects within and around systems theory include complexity, self-organization, connectionism, and adaptive systems in the 1940s and 1950s. The term goes back to von Bertalanffy's 1968 book titled *General System Theory*.[2]

My former business partner, Ian Hathaway, spent the past few years searching for effective models for startup communities and entrepreneurial ecosystems. These are discussed in great detail in his and Brad's book, *The Startup Community Way*. Their conclusion? The science of systems theory is the best means by which to understand the dynamics of startup communities.

Stay with me here. I know this sounds academic, but I'll explain it in simple terms so you can apply systems theory to your community-building efforts. It's critical that you take what will possibly be a counterintuitive examination of your and your community's approach to ecosystem building.

---

1   Wikipedia, s.v. "Systems Theory," last modified January 27, 2023, https://en.wikipedia.org/wiki/Systems_theory#General_systems_research_and_systems_inquiry.

2   Ludwig von Bertalanffy, *General System Theory: Foundations, Development, Applications*, rev. ed. (New York: George Braziller Inc., 1969).

Most systems theory advocates outline different types of subsystems:

- Ordered | Unordered, or
- Simple | Complicated | Complex

For startup community building and this field guide, we are going to use the SIMPLE | COMPLICATED | COMPLEX mode to simplify this even more and provide an example of each:

- A simple system is like a recipe for a meal. We know all the ingredients (variables), we understand the interactions between all the variables, and we have a clear set of rules or processes to follow. In a simple system there is a high level of predictability as to the outcome (i.e., twenty chefs with the same ingredients following the same process should produce the same meal).
- A complicated system is like sending a rocket to the moon. The first launch is very difficult; the following launches become a bit easier, but predictability still varies. This system requires an inordinate amount of time identifying the many variables and an intense amount of time understanding how those variables interact with one another. Think about engineering and reverse engineering to achieve a difficult but a more predictable outcome.
- A complex system is like raising a child. In this system, we do not know all the variables that create the outcome, and we certainly don't understand how the same variables seem to interact to create different outcomes. Anyone with multiple children or siblings innately understands this. Even with the same parents, house, food, school, family, etc., two children turn out to be complete opposites. Outcomes in complex systems are unpredictable.

My methodology is based on the science of systems theory, specifically complex adaptive systems, where the focus is on connectivity, human interaction, and experimentation. We believe that the understanding and practice of entrepreneurial ecosystem building can be improved by incorporating insights from complex systems—a "science" used to explain the dynamics of physical, biological, social, and information networks. But you first must understand the differences between complicated systems and complex systems.

Complicated systems have a specific goal in mind, where leaders strive to engineer an outcome through problem-solving, structured organization, and programming.

Qualities of complicated systems include the following:

- Identifying and utilizing expertise to effectively reverse engineer problems
- Striving for a repeatable and predictable set of processes
- Implementing a top-down hierarchical approach to managing interactions between community actors

Large corporations and government institutions are perfect examples of entities that optimize for a complicated approach. Most executives in these types of organizations have built up complicated leadership muscles to bring success to these entities.

However, this is the wrong approach when developing or growing an entrepreneurial ecosystem.

Here are a few reasons why:

- Your customers are the entrepreneurs, not your shareholders or stakeholders. By definition, entrepreneurs are disruptors of the status quo, hierarchy, and structure.
- Entrepreneurs are inspired by other entrepreneurs. Non-entrepreneurs just don't get it. So if non-entrepreneurs take leadership positions, the real entrepreneurs fade out of the community.
- Non-entrepreneur-led initiatives typically don't address the real issues needed to create startup progress.
- Hierarchical community structures create friction against getting things done.
- Top-down methodologies create an ownership attitude, which again does not match the community approach. There can never be a CEO of the startup community.
- A complicated approach to building or growing a startup community is based on the assumption that there is one way to go forward (a plan, a recipe, or a detailed playbook). Subsequent activities will then serve that notion and they will ultimately not work for your community.

Warning: just about every businessperson outside of the entrepreneurs will want to pigeonhole the process into a top-down approach. They'll try to figure out who the "leader" is; they'll want to know how success is measured; they'll be interested in specific outcomes on a quarterly basis. Truthfully, no judgment here as everything we're taught, and nearly every company, church, and nonprofit (even AYSO Soccer for kids), is organized as a complicated system. It's how we were taught to view the world.

A more appropriate approach to entrepreneurial ecosystems is to view the ecosystem as a complex system. Complexity results from the interrelationship, interaction, and interconnectivity of elements within a system and between a system and its environment.[3]

Qualities of complex systems include the following:

- Members encourage meaningful interactions through organized as well as serendipitous collisions.
- There is no one leader, and those who take leadership positions do not attempt to control outcomes.
- It's a bottom-up approach where each actor is a full member of the community.
- Members strive for guidelines versus rules.
- Members can take on multiple roles and play them when they choose.

If entrepreneurial ecosystems are complex systems, then by definition an entrepreneurial ecosystem *cannot be engineered*; there's no leader assigning tasks, there's no master plan to execute, and methods for measuring accountability and outcomes are not easily identified or agreed upon. For many of you, this notion goes against every muscle you've built over your career. Your success is the direct result of building plans, assigning tasks, and driving accountability through metrics and KPIs. It's also the way most of us went through school, from kindergarten to wherever we ended up: the teacher provides the content, we memorize it, get tested on it, then get evaluated on it. Education is nearly always "engineered" through textbooks, lectures, tests, etc.

---

3   Serena Chan, "Complex Adaptive Systems" (working paper, ESD.83 Research Seminar in Engineering Systems, MIT, October 31, 2001/November 6, 2001), https://web.mit.edu/esd.83/www/notebook/Complex%20Adaptive%20Systems.pdf.

Still not convinced? Then let me ask you a simple question. If there's a master plan to execute that can be modified to your region, and if the only barriers to executing this master plan are time and money, and if I told you that to date local enthusiasts just like you have spent billions of dollars to execute said master plan, then... Why aren't there over two hundred Silicon Valleys today? I can promise you it's not for lack of motivation or money. I would share that it has been a lack of the right mindset or framework that has held well-intentioned leaders back from accelerating their community forward.

Endeavor Insight's October 2018 report titled *Fostering Productive Entrepreneurship Communities* analyzed two basic approaches: bottom up and top down.[4] This is summarized nicely in the following chart.

COMMON APPROACHES OBSERVED IN ENTREPRENEURSHIP COMMUNITIES

BOTTOM-UP APPROACHES for Supporting Local Entrepreneurs	TOP-DOWN APPROACHES for Supporting Local Entrepreneurs
LEADERSHIP & FINANCING:	
Objectives are identified by leaders of local companies that reached scale	**Objectives** are identified by people outside the community with little-to-no participation by local entrepreneurial leaders
Ongoing decision-making authority includes a significant number of top-performing founders, though others can be involved as well	**Ongoing decision-making authority** excludes leaders of local companies that reached scale and often rests outside the community
Funding includes tangible contributions from leaders of local entrepreneurial companies	**Funding** comes primarily from outside of the entrepreneurship community
RESULTS:	
Elevates the influence of people with experience scaling local companies: typically successful local entrepreneurs or emigrants from the community who are successful founders elsewhere	**Elevates** the influence of people without experience scaling local companies: typically expats or local residents with no record of entrepreneurial success

Source: Endeavor Insight.

4   Rhett Morris and Lili Török, *Fostering Productive Entrepreneurship Communities: Key Lessons on Generating Jobs, Economic Growth, and Innovation* (Endeavor Insight, October 2018), https://endeavor.org/wp-content/uploads/2021/09/Fostering-Productive-Entrepreneurship-Communities.pdf.

STARTUP COMMUNITY BUILDING IS FOR EVERYONE! (IS THIS YOU?)

Some of the first questions you may ask are:

- "Is this something I can get involved in?"
- "Am I allowed to play a part in this?"
- "Can I coordinate an activity to help without getting permission?"

The unequivocal and simple answer to all of these is YES, YES, YES!

Great startup communities are inclusive of anyone who wants to help play a role regardless of the size of the activity. Great startup communities do not judge, curate, or play the role of gatekeeper—there is no CEO or king of the startup community. In fact, the best communities are more like networks of fellow tribesmen, not a hierarchical structure with assigned roles. Lastly, driven by the flat, network-like structure, there is no one you need to get permission from to participate.

Let's take a look at some of the most common members of the startup community:

1. Entrepreneurs/Founders: The core of the community, these are the women and men who are currently building their companies. I see them as all in, and by that I mean that they're 100 percent dedicated to their startups. Though there is never enough time in the day to accomplish even 10 percent of what their companies need, they somehow also find time to play a role in their communities. More on that later.
2. Individual Community Enthusiasts: These are active play-

ers and see something missing, so they jump in and play a role. These could be employees of a firm (not the founder) or even retired. Individual community enthusiasts may run a solo consulting practice.

3. **Entrepreneur Supporter Organizations (ESOs):** No decent-sized city in this world lacks some type of ESO. These organizations are made up of some of the most passionate people I've ever met. Some of their work is paid for or subsidized by government, foundations, and corporations, and some individuals pay out of their own pockets. Their support is usually packaged into programming to address the needs of new and scaling startup companies and their founders.

4. **Government (City, State, or Federal) Administrators:** As the importance of a robust startup community becomes better known, we see the emergence of government as a driver of activities. This is generally good, but each government actor must understand how best to play their support role. *The Startup Community Way* does a great job of outlining the attitudes required to be effective.

5. **Universities/Colleges:** Even the smallest towns or cities typically have a college or university, and I have yet to find one where someone isn't advocating some type of entrepreneurship as part of their offerings. This includes instructors/professors, researchers, program leaders, organizers, and endowments. And don't forget the students.

6. **Public-Private Partnerships:** Every day there seems to be a new organization that combines these two seemingly opposing entities. The best version utilizes the public dollars available but operates in a nimbler, hopefully faster, and ultimately more impactful way. More and more, these public-private organizations are joining the startup community ranks.

7. **Community Foundations:** One of the more interesting finds, these nonprofit organizations usually have a charter to help the community. Many are oriented to underserved populations, but some extend that definition and mission to entrepreneurship.

8. **Local Business Mavens (individuals, not the entity):** The motivation for these leaders is pure—they're ready to give back to the community that hosted their success. Many of them have significant charity programs, but this is different. This is real investment either in space, local funds, or even local companies.

9. **Corporations and Their Executives:** Every company is a tech company (or so says Marc Andreessen, founder of Netscape, father of the modern internet, and noted venture capitalist). To that end, every company is challenged to remain innovative. As talent acquisition gets harder and harder, smart and forward-thinking local businesses are looking to find ways to address their innovation and talent needs and are looking to the local startup community.

10. **Successful Founders:** Many communities have at least one person who started, grew, and reaped a large financial reward for their company-building efforts. As founders who lived the journey and have that native DNA that inherently wants to give back to other founders, successful founders typically are willing to help grow their startup community.

11. **Investors:** Successful investors implicitly understand that a strong community yields better founders and companies and better investment opportunities. Many carve out time and effort to engage in and drive specific activities outside of their day jobs.

12. **Vendors:** "Send lawyers, guns, and money, the shit has hit the fan," sang Warren Zevon to some of us back in the sev-

enties. Accountants and lawyers are just two of a growing group of future ecosystem contributors and partners of the community. Yes, their interest has an element of self-service, but I've witnessed firsthand the leadership that a veteran startup lawyer elicits when removing their self-interest and signing up for the greater mission of the community.

13. **Alumni. Boomerangers. Expatriates:** These are people who grew up or went to college in your town, or their spouse did. Whatever the driver, they're back, and they bring a lot of entrepreneurial expertise from elsewhere. If that experience is from Silicon Valley, New York City, or a similar leading startup community, then they have even more to share with their newly adopted towns.

14. **Media:** Think broadly. I'm not just thinking about traditional media here. I'm thinking more about web, email, and social media storytelling that shares the narrative arcs of companies in the startup community. Some of these leaders and their platforms are as impactful if not more impactful than other more obvious actors and platforms.

SO, YOU'RE A COMMUNITY BUILDER?

I think it's always important to understand *why* people choose to step up and contribute. As my longest-running mentor, Bart Faber, once told me, "Business is about leverage. You either have it or you have to create it." Understanding motivation is a key element in creating leverage. And applied leverage helps you get things done.

Let's start with me as our first example. I am an entrepreneur. I am an investor. But my motivations have a different spin that's not related to those roles. I love the idea of solving a complex problem. I also get energy from helping others. Frankly, it's a bit selfish on my part. It's an itch I have to scratch. I'm also comfortable filling leadership voids when I know I can play that role and make an impact.

One of the most common motivations for getting involved in a startup community is the very idea that a more robust, larger community will eventually bring good things to me, my company, my organization, and my community. Think about a founder of a company co-leading a group of community leaders as they stand up an event that recruits secondary offices of larger companies to their city.

In the early days of the Raleigh-Durham startup community growth, I was frequently asked if I would represent the community when the local chamber folks were recruiting a company to the area. Why would I spend the time? New companies bring talent, money, energy, and the storyline that my community is on its way up. There's a natural flywheel effect that perpetuates the idea of locating there and getting access to our resources. That in turn creates a positive contagion that spreads through the community, which reinforces the notion. Why would they ask me? I am a serial entrepreneur with a large success under my belt (MapQuest). That is sexy to some. Plus I am VERY passionate about my community and share that enthusiastically.

Pure unadulterated economic development drives many a government leader or quasi-government leader. It's their job as well as their reason for existing. This motivation is growing across the world as many now realize the benefits of a robust startup community that I outlined earlier.

Building a startup community or entrepreneurial ecosystem can be a job. In fact, more and more organizations are being created to facilitate and manage programs and activities. These mostly nonprofits have the pressure of raising money for their organizations, which many times conflicts with their stated goal of serving entrepreneurs. This pressure can result in an organization and its staff being more focused on staying afloat and keeping their jobs than supporting founders.

Capitalism is a driver for many of us—entrepreneurship is fertile ground for generating income. Vendors including lawyers, accountants, marketing firms, and development agencies are businesses themselves with revenue and profit incentives.

Being a member of a startup community means access to a weird tribe of enthusiastic, passionate, living-on-the-edge-type people. Like rock stars and sports celebrities, people want to be in their orbit. Being close to the action and finding ways to individually support their journeys only adds to the excitement of participation.

Novel and unique approaches to problem-solving drive many entrepreneurs. The whole concept of doing something that has never been done before is a wicked motivator. Involvement in community building offers a similar energy. Creativity is a drug in itself, regardless of where or how it's applied. Its application in problem-solving around a startup community can be a double-whammy shot of high-octane fuel to the soul.

I find that the desire for more entrepreneurs and even more successful entrepreneurs in your city can be a mission for some people. It certainly is an admirable position to rally around.

This "do good" mentality is similar to other charitable programs that citizens get behind, but with an economic impact. I want to work with people who have a sense of mission—they belong to something bigger than themselves. Foreshadowing moment: surrounding yourself with these types of people or converting folks to adopt this line of thinking is what supercharges a startup community.

ARE YOU READY TO PLAY AN IMPACTFUL ROLE IN YOUR COMMUNITY?

So, maybe you don't see yourself in one of these archetypal roles I listed above.

Or, maybe you think that your community is different from the ones I used as examples.

Or, maybe you are not sure if you have anything to offer your community.

Well, if you came this far, I can assure you that your community is no different from the ones I talked about, and there is a place for you, because there's always a place for the motivated. As I navigate around the world, working directly with people exactly like you, I get enthused with the idea that there's another emerging leader ready to step up and help entrepreneurs achieve success. What better mission can there be but to be a positive part of someone else's life journey?

It is this simple idea that I want you to carry forward. Great communities welcome new actors who are ready to augment what's happening today. In fact, they seek and support new actors with the idea that they can only add to the resources available to entrepreneurs. Think like a ten-year-old. Can you have a great game of kickball with three or four kids? No, you want as many kids as possible.

I also realize that if you are reading this book, your community probably has a lot of work left to do. And I understand that with those gaps and voids, some may view your idea as "not the way we do it around here" or push back with "we've never tried anything like that." Don't fret. This is normal. As I've shared with hundreds of you, "Same problems, different weather."

Well, buckle up your shoes and put your big person's pants on because it is time for you to channel your inner entrepreneur. It is time to put yourself out there just like the founders you wish to serve. It is time for you to make the community builder leap.

CHAPTER 2

BUILDING PRINCIPLES

The fort-building story is a simple parable that's rich with lessons to apply to your own startup community–building journey. Startups are hard. Community building is even harder. I trust that we all know that by now. Standing up new activities without knowing what will work is frightening, and so is getting support from people you don't know. Finding a way to build trust in a group that doesn't have the time to evaluate your motives is almost impossible.

Five basic areas of fort building closely align with building a startup community. *Build the Fort: Startup Community Builder's Field Guide* outlines these five basic elements. They are simple to understand and provide a great foundation for a successful journey.

In this book you will learn how to achieve these five elements:

1. Identify, Recruit, and Influence All of the Actors in the Ecosystem
2. Partner or Team with Skilled and Trustworthy Peers

3. Assess and Leverage the Community Assets Closest to You
4. Create a Short-Term-Win Mindset to Drive Confidence
5. Build Your Community without Inhibition, Permission, or Data

Not sure or don't fully understand? Go out and watch a group of ten- to twelve-year-olds interact on a project. Going from idea to partner to tasks to outcome is so easy for them.

What are the types of outcomes that you and your community should aspire to achieve? Said another way, what goals should you set for your community? Like many complex systems, the goals and subsequent outcomes are not always easy to identify, encourage, or achieve.

As you begin to rally the troops or inject yourself into the community leadership, it will be important for you and others to fully embrace the ten-year-old simplicity of building a fort (while setting simple goals and outcomes).

Let's get started and see where the lessons learned from my then ten-year-old friend Jimmy Doyle, as well as my community-building experience, can help you become your best startup community leader.

PRINCIPLE #1: IDENTIFY ALL ACTORS

Step one in fort building is getting out and meeting people. Startup communities are made up of people, so "yous gots to go to da people"! No other way around it. And you need to talk to lots of individuals who are playing many different roles. Way too many times I see current leaders, new leaders, and consultants come in and talk to all the ESO managers. THIS IS WRONG! You miss the whole point if you don't take to the streets and talk to founders.

The good news is that they are all looking for help. All you have to do is find them. You need about four to five target people to get started. Networking 101 is that each one of those targets will connect you with three others; your first five will quickly turn into fifteen.

From there I look for ways to get warm introductions to those people. I can speak from personal experience of the increased response rates from a warm introduction. Your story is simple and is easily activated: "I'm new to town and hoping to get engaged with entrepreneurs, investors, and supporters of the local ecosystem so I can give back a little. I see you know Jerry—mind making an introduction?" I actually kept a spreadsheet of the targets who introduced me and when I followed up, when we met, etc.

I make it easy to connect by offering to come by their local coffee shop, frosty beverage provider, or lunch hangout. In every city there are a handful of places where entrepreneurs hang out. Meet there and you're bound to get introduced to two or three other people in the community—and the spider web of contacts quickly builds.

Like any good discovery interview, you should spend as much time listening as you do talking. You just need to lead with: "I'm hoping to give back and support whatever current efforts are underway."

Your ideas on how to further serve or augment the current activities across the community can come later. Right now you're mapping the who, what, where of the startup community. It's critical that you ask three questions at the end of the half-hour coffee:

1. Is there anything I can do to support your efforts with regard to either your business or the startup community?
2. Who else should I be connecting with?
3. Mind making intros to your three closest entrepreneur friends?

Communities are made up of lots of different actors, so it's important that you meet a cross section of them. Most important are the entrepreneurs, yet they will be the hardest to connect with. With them, you'll have to make it abundantly clear that you're here to help them and that you're not selling anything.

What do you have to offer them? It's more than you think!

- **Contact list:** Everyone needs new connections; your network is new to the area.
- **Experiences:** You've seen things and done things that nobody there has done; that is special and valuable to the community.
- **Creative ideas on how to help:** Here I'm referring to their company or entity as well as the community.
- **New energy:** Positive only, please! This is not the time to be critical or judgmental.

Pretty quickly you'll begin to hear the same names offered up, and when you meet these entrepreneurs, you'll pick up on the ones who exhibit natural and obvious influence. Those will be your super nodes. Life just got a whole lot easier.

PRINCIPLE #2: PARTNER

When you're ten, the idea of a partner is pretty simple. We were so in the moment at that age, and looking back, that seemed to make life much easier. Things seem to change pretty dramatically by the time we get to be adults. It feels like as adults we've lost that innocence that enabled us to move quickly with no baggage and traded it for safety, protection, and an attempt to manage our fears.

When Jimmy, Danny, Timmy (my fellow fort builders), and I agreed to work together we had something already built in: we had a level of trust.[5] Now, don't get me wrong—it was a ten-year-old's trust. But to us it was just as important as adult trust. Trust is a fickle beast, is it not? It has layers to it, and though it takes a long time to add them, removing them can happen much more quickly.

One of the things I want you to think about is whether you have too high of a filter, an almost impermeable layer, to your trust. I know that as adults we have this filter—but is it preventing us from doing what we dream about getting done? I think so, and this is the heart of channeling your inner ten-year-old.

In my fort-building story, there was a subtle but important concept that comes naturally to kids but not so much to adults: we teamed up. Why? One, it was a lot more fun doing something with someone than going solo. Two, we got to use each other as mini sounding boards. We intrinsically knew that we didn't know all the answers. We needed one another. Our initial idea

---

5   Learn more about Chris's fellow fort builders in his other book, *Build the Fort: Why 5 Simple Lessons You Learned as a 10 year-old Can Set You Up for Startup Success* (Bracey, VA: Lisa Hagan Books, 2015).

for a fort was quickly improved by others—a wall here, a door there. It was through the actual fort building that trust was established; the fort then became "ours."

In startup community building we talk about "meaningful connections." As kids we built these connections in hours, if not minutes—as adults it seems to take weeks or even months. I find that way too many of us miss opportunities to uncover a new partner under the guise of safety. What if we could channel our inner ten-year-old selves? You know that kid. He was the one who said, "Sure, I'll build a fort with you!" without hesitation.

The word *meaningful* has a pretty broad definition, but let me share one concept that encapsulates the spirit of the word: #givefirst. Popularized by Brad Feld over a decade ago, #give-first means that you are willing to give of your time, your brain, and your network without expecting anything in return. It's the opposite of the transaction mentality so commonplace in business.

Those of us who live by the #givefirst credo find partners easily and often. Giving without expectations quickly builds trust and credibility. You want to help your community? How about finding someone else's project and offering to help? My long-time friend Marshall Clark would run the popcorn machine at my circus-themed job fair. Megan Carriker would curate articles for my volunteer-model startup community blog. Joe Queenan volunteered to help me bring a new mindset to Columbia, South Carolina. Each one of those actions signaled to me that they wanted to support my project. The result? Credibility and trust. I would do anything for any of them today.

These are meaningful connections. They are gold to us individually, and they're gold to the community. The cumulative effect of a group of leaders exhibiting a #givefirst mentality and setting that principle as a community norm is powerful. As a community, we publicly demonstrate what we value. Others, such as those on the periphery of the community (either recently engaged or new to the area), then readily view #givefirst as the way this community operates. And a positive new community norm begins, which is reinforced by every new #givefirst action.

But many still keep a scorecard. They live in a transactional world. I hate this world. It consumes too much energy that could best be put to use elsewhere. What to do about these people? I can assure you that they're part of your community. Start by sharing what you believe in and how you operate. Leaders can publicly support #givefirst as the community norm by blogging, speaking, and doing the panel thing at meetups. Plus, it's another way to find trustworthy partners.

One of the simplest ways to help someone is to introduce them to others in your network. My logic train goes like this:

- You need something to get your project ahead.
- You don't have that thing readily available to you.
- Thus you need help from someone else.
- You need access to people who can help you with that thing.
- You need to find out who they are.
- You then need to be connected with them.
- You want those connections to be frictionless.

A transactional mindset would have you start down this path when you need it. A #givefirst mindset says that you build a network by helping others, so when you need something, that network is there for you. In other words, you've already invested in it.

I find that there are enablers and there are users of the community. I can share that it is a lot more fun to be an enabler than a user. To see someone else's passion project soar is a special feeling. Try supporting two or three projects in your community without any hooks. What is there to lose?

Which projects should you support? Great question. Let's take you back to our first principle of identifying and recruiting all ecosystem actors. I asked that you connect with as large a number of people as you can manage. I think twenty to forty should be a target over a few months. During this time you will undoubtedly find people you like enough, people who don't light your fire, and a handful that feel like family. You know the feeling I am talking about. You go home to your spouse or roommate and share, "I just met my brother from another mother, or a sister from another mister." These are special moments and you cannot let them just fade away. They need to be activated and they need to be activated right away. Grab these as they don't come every day or every month. There is a very good chance that these are your future trustworthy partners.

My last point here is about the diversity of your approach. Diversity comes in many packages—not just skin color. There's gender diversity, education diversity, age diversity, and diversity of thought. I like to think that we want to be diverse in our approach, but let's be honest: we typically gravitate toward those who look like us. No judgment here. But I will ask you this simple question: what do you miss when you overly constrain your network or community? You'll never know exactly, but I can tell you from personal experience that if you constrain your network you will have fewer opportunities.

True community leadership comes from the people who naturally operate with a #givefirst attitude and build meaningful connections regardless of where their new peer partners come from.

PRINCIPLE #3: ASSESS AND LEVERAGE ASSETS

When we agreed to build a fort, the first thing we had to determine was what we had to work with and what our long-term vision was. We agreed on a location and chimed in with what types of materials we had at our disposal. After that discussion, we quickly and frictionlessly assigned one another a few tasks. There weren't good tasks and nasty tasks, just things to get done. There were no arguments and no negotiating, per se. Just a simple divide and conquer.

So, what are the assets for community building? More importantly, what are the assets that are closest to you that you may be able to leverage?

Since communities are made up of people, I would start here. People are the biggest asset in a startup community. Earlier, I laid out all of the different actors who play a role. Though all of them are important, there are a few who play an outsize role and your job is to find out who they are. I have encouraged you to cast a wide net and socialize with as many diverse people as possible, and I have pushed you to build some meaningful relationships with as many as makes sense.

In this world, I frequently talk about leaders and influencers. I encourage you to view these as two distinct groups. To best understand the difference, head to the back of the book to the definitions appendix. (I told you it was boring but important, so go back right now if you need to—I'll wait right here.) It turns out you need both. Focus just on leaders and you'll lose credibility among entrepreneurs. Ignore the leaders and you risk alienating a group that has the ability to fund, convene, and empower others.

Here, I will build upon the notion of identifying leaders and influencers and throw in a little wrinkle. Your job is to figure out what assets you need for getting your vision off the ground. Whereas before I wanted you to find like-minded folks to partner with, here I want you to find people to help you get things done. They're not necessarily one and the same, and understanding the difference is critical.

Generally you need stuff (wood, nails, tarps) to build a fort. What is the stuff you need to be an effective community leader? Community leaders are an important ingredient in this recipe. Leaders have access to things you don't have, including the following:

- **Credibility:** By default, nobody knows who you are or what your agenda is. But everyone knows the local leaders and influencers. Bringing them into your orbit and your project gives you credibility. Lots of things help build credibility, and I give you a tool kit full of them later in the book. For now, realize that you need to build clout with local leaders and influencers.
- **Relationships:** By nature, leaders have large and impactful

networks. You don't get to their position without it. From that one person at the university who can sign off on hosting an event there, to the local microbrewery owner who's looking for any opportunity to build brand awareness, leaders have relationships you need.

- **Databases:** Generally I think in terms of listservs here, but you can also insert social media. Email is still one of the most effective ways to reach people. Local lists are like gold, and starting out, you got nothing. But you'll need to message a large local group of people, and your new leader/influencer friends have easy access to them.
- **Space:** One of the most effective community-building tools is to convene people. For that to happen you need space, and preferably for free. A corporate board room, a university hall, or the back room of a coffee shop are all great destinations.
- **Money:** Ahhh, the gasoline that makes the car move. I list money almost last, as I want you to think about non-monetary ways to knock out what you need to get done. However, some projects require money. And some leaders have access to money, or access to others who have money.
- **Stuff:** I love this word. In this category, I'm thinking of all the things besides space and money. These can include A/V equipment, beer, coffee and food, signage, advertisements, furniture, notable speakers, apartments, travel subsidies—the list goes on.
- **Time:** I'm referring to *their* time. Probably the most valuable asset they have that you need.

These seven assets typify what you need to get a community-building project off the ground.

The good news is that most of the leaders in town are in their positions because they like to get things done too. In Buffalo, New York, Eric Reich is CEO and founder of Campus Labs but also served as chairman of 43N, which serves entrepreneurs. In Fort Wayne, Indiana, Crystal Vann Wallstrom led the charge in transforming an old GE plant as it morphs into the region's largest innovation hub. In Cleveland, Ohio, Ed Buchholz founded ExpenseBot but also spends visible time pushing the entrepreneur agenda hard. In Lima, Peru, Andres Benavides is a passionate twenty-something who, through his role in the federal government, set up many programs, including one of the most inspiring entrepreneur conferences in Latin America I've ever been a part of.

Leaders come in all shapes and sizes (and roles, ages, gender). It is not hard to find these leaders. All of them make themselves available. A simple web search or a few questions to a handful of related individuals should do the trick.

So connect with them (if you haven't already) and ask them for help. Simple as that. Like Jimmy and me asking Danny and Timmy to help, reach out and tell them what you need. I promise you that they are as interested in what you're doing as you are.

If that's the easy part, here comes the hard part: you'll need to build your own trust and credibility. This doesn't happen overnight, even if you had that trust in a previous role, company, or community.

By spring of 2010, I had spent about six months building momentum for my accelerator idea. I met with at least 275 community members one on one. For many of them, I made subsequent introductions or served them in some capacity. I'd stood up two founder events (eighty people attended the first, 120 the second). Though I hadn't acquired a place to convene, I had a conversation with a real estate leader who was interested in creating a startup space. The only thing left was to raise funds for the community to stand up my original accelerator, the Triangle Startup Factory.

While I trolled the area for funds, the heads of existing entrepreneurial organizations stood there in what I would call a passive-aggressive stance. They offered to help me raise money by giving me a list of people who typically invested—but didn't provide email addresses or phone numbers, much less a warm introduction. A few months later they convened a meeting of these local players to determine my fate; however, I was not invited to speak. (I now know this to have been the last vestige of the region's "old boys' club.")

It didn't really matter what the outcome of that meeting was going to be. For the past six months, I had created meaningful relationships with founders and community members. Over that time, I had exhibited #givefirst qualities that built trust.

Many in that room and more across the region had a distaste for and were not supportive of the closed-door nature of that meeting, and they rallied around me. Things were changing, and a lot of folks liked the more open and transparent community approach.

I share that story for a number of reasons, but the important one in this context is that you will need to build credibility to get through the pressures of the old guard. You may find that credibility early, or you may find it late, like I did. But rest assured, it will come. To be successful, you'll need to push through the barriers and friction that come with creating change.

And don't worry, the landscape of activities and events related to entrepreneurship won't be barren after your informal survey and first set of meetings. Things will indeed be going on.

Some of those existing activities might be looking a little tired. They may need new speakers, a format refresh, or a brilliant tactic to generate new participants. You'll also find gaps in the offerings that could inspire new activity among the many actors in the ecosystem.

I summarize this mindset as such. You can

1. lead new activities solo,
2. augment current activities, or
3. partner to drive new activities.

PRINCIPLE #4: APPLY A SHORT-TERM MINDSET

One reason that fort building is simple as a kid is that the tasks are pretty simple and the rules are easy to understand. First, the rules (if there are any) are either known or the implication is obvious. Second, the rules are enforced every day, mostly in an implied manner. The basic kid-oriented fort-building rules are these:

1. Don't be a jerk. Kids have no tolerance for jerks.
2. It has to be fun. No fun? No can do.
3. Nobody is the boss. There can be leadership and innate collaboration, but don't tell one another what to do.

4. The tasks have to be commensurate with the value. In a fort-building context, the end result better be measured in one to two days (any longer and it's not worth it) and the tasks need to be in line with the value of a fort.
5. These are four simple-to-understand rules for fort building.

The unspoken lesson learned is that the kids built the fort together as a team. The fort is theirs. They designed it, acquired the parts, and put it together as a group (as opposed to having a parent buy the fort on Amazon). Or in startup community parlance, an ill-conceived fort was not handed to them by a bunch of well-meaning businesspeople or bureaucrats who've never used a fort before.

In startup community building, one of the first things you can do is understand the basic rules. Here are my rules (borrowed liberally from Brad's *Startup Communities* book—the Boulder Thesis) for startup communities:

1. Founders are the center of all activity. Non-entrepreneurs serve entrepreneurs.
2. Communities are inclusive of anyone who wants to play a role.
3. No one owns the community. There is no CEO.
4. The community mission comes before my own personal or business or organizational agenda.

Take a second and juxtapose the fort-building rules with the community-building rules. There's a clear and overlapping spirit in both that resonates. It is the idea that I come after something bigger than myself, my needs, my goals, my aspirations, my desire—all of these are secondary to the community. It's that selfless approach, the belief that a rising tide raises all boats, that applies to community building. If you, or the people in your community-building effort, are just participating to get the most out of the community for yourself, it'll never work. It's doomed for failure. The people with the assets will step away, the leaders will stop coming to meetings, the free space you found when you got started will now require a lease, the university that provided a forum will close its doors. Most importantly, the very founders you wish to serve won't make time for this selfless activity. This is especially difficult with today's me-first mentality.

The title of this section—Apply A Short-Term Mindset—has three ideas, and each is meant to connote a tighter meaning. Let's start with "short-term." This may seem to be counter to the notion that startup community building is a generational journey, but I don't think so. Try this on for size: consider your task to be similar to the mantra "Think Global, Act Local." Our version might be something like "Have the patience of a long-term outlook, but get shit done today!"

Startup community building—with a selfless mindset—is all about momentum. Small, seemingly inconsequential wins add up to something special—each one builds micro-contagions that help spread good mojo. And short-term focus enables each of us to make an impact now. Spending too much time wondering what the long-term results might be only drains us of the physical and mental energy we need now.

When kids are building a fort, they aren't thinking of the next few forts and whether the current design will be conducive for adding a bathroom ten years from now. Their focus is on one to three days max. When you spend most of your energy on the short term, you make the types of decisions that maximize your efforts right then; you defer the decisions that can paralyze you or the team.

A few community leaders were having a beer at one of our ad hoc late-in-the-day meetings when someone brought up the idea of a small festival, suggesting that it "could be our version of SXSW." This concept has probably been advocated in just about every city in the US over the last twenty years, and we were no different.

Except that we went ahead and pulled something together and launched Paradoxos—"absurd yet seemingly true"—to celebrate startups, music, and food. Year one had around four hundred attendees. Year two had twelve hundred. We had no illusions that this would turn into anything big. Our soft commitment to one another would be that we would work together on this for at least five years. We weren't afraid to start small and see where it went.

After two years, a larger event from across the state came to us and asked if we'd like to combine efforts. They desired our tech vibe and community. The Moog Festival was recast a year later with over eight thousand attendees from around the world. The light that this festival shined on our city and our startup community remains bright today. All of that light started with a beer among a handful of professional friends deciding to do something together.

I would like to reiterate that there is no recipe for success. There is, however, a mindset you can deploy (selfless, short-term focus, gathering of assets, experiments and iteration). So, again, while there isn't a recipe, a person or a community can follow these guidelines and increase their success after applying the principles in this book.

Everything you do in terms of startup community building is an experiment, and experiments fail—that is why we call them experiments. This is certainly true with events, which seem to have a given life span. There's excitement for the first few, and then somehow it begins to fade away. This is okay. The event served a purpose for a while and now needs to be replaced with something new that addresses the needs of today's community members. Things invariably change, which reinforces my argument that you're better off focusing on the short-term benefit of your idea. Just get it done with the assets you have now.

I generally think an informal stance is more appropriate than a formal one. Think more roll-up-your-sleeves than strategic planning documents. More ad hoc, as-needed meetings rather than scheduled affairs. Think more meeting-of-the-motivated than named-group-with-officers. And think about people more as opting in rather than being assigned a task or mission. At Techstars we called this a GSD mentality, which is GET SHIT DONE.

Along that same mindset is the idea that we are all equals and that there are no VIPs. This concept supports our network-versus-hierarchical community structure point of view. That's why there shouldn't be officers of the community or anyone else walking around like royalty. The only royalty in the startup community are the founders who are giving back to their community every day. But most of them will not want to wear that crown—nor should they.

A collective is a group of people acting in concert with one another on a common goal. I like the perception of the word *collective*. Startup communities are much closer to a collective than a distinct entity.

In terms of the startup community, not getting this mindset correct is where the wheels fall off the startup community bus almost every time. Do you and the other drivers of the community have a truly "collective" purpose? In every community I've served, I've observed a mixed set of purposes. Mixed or alternative goals are another inhibitor to progress.

Some of us are driven by greed. Some by fame. Some have a mission, and some want to serve themselves. You'll find people who have to have control and others who easily release control. Some know better and some don't care. Somehow these all seem like adult issues, something we would never find in fort building as ten-year-olds.

As you prepare to play a more active role in your startup community and put in place some of the ideas floating around in your head, stop, look in the mirror, and ask yourself whether you're signing up for a collective purpose or driving your own agenda. The answer will dictate your near- and long-term success. You can be fruitful in the near term with your own agenda; you cannot be successful in the long term without a collective purpose.

You need look no further than a handful of local startups to find a model and an example of this playing out in real time. As Steve Jobs once said, "Startups suffer from indigestion, not starvation." What he meant was that there are too many ideas, paths, visions; it is taking all of these into account and finding the right idea, path and vision.

Startup communities have plenty of ideas/activities/goals; they typically suffer from too many fragmented approaches or goals. These are always driven by a lack of common or collective purpose. These conflicting activities are driven by actors operating in a vacuum, typically with a mindset of wanting to control everything. Fragmented approaches are nearly always due to an unwillingness to collaborate (and many times ego and selfish actions).

What I think is interesting is that startups suffer from the same issue, which is why I think they're a fantastic petri dish to examine. I mean, if you can't find a startup to evaluate while you're working for your startup community, then you're out of touch. And if you're out of touch, don't worry. All you have to do is join a meetup, go to a chamber of commerce meeting and ask around, go to your local accounting or law firm and ask about startups, and look online in your community. There are lots of ways to figure out the state of your local ecosystem.

Collective is the how, but purpose is the why.

For the four boys who were building a fort, the purpose was simple and apparent. There was no need to overcomplicate the goal. We simply wanted a fort to play in.

Your startup community will need to form a purpose. Later in the book, I will outline some of the ways you can do this, but for now let's focus on why we need a purpose and what a few examples of a startup community purpose look like.

Step one on our collective purpose is to separate the tasks from the purpose. They are completely different animals, so let's recognize that right now. Our purpose has to be bigger than the tasks, activities, events, and fundraising that sit in front of us. It has to be that one thing that binds us all together.[6] Purpose is that thing that is bigger than any one of us. And we sign up for a purpose every day, whether we know it or not.

Purpose is that feeling where you're willing to do something for the betterment of the community and not yourself. You do this with your family. You do this with some of your hobbies. You do this when driving your car and following the rules of the road.

Earlier I spoke about the startup tribe. The reason I love the word *tribe* is that it implies purpose. We're part of the startup community. We believe that a stronger startup community yields benefits to us as individuals, it benefits the people in our community, and it benefits future generations. In this sense, we believe that the community is more important than us.

If you are lucky or good enough to have formed a collective purpose in your startup community, your next step is to develop its clear and compelling definition.

But let's first look at a few startup community purposes that *don't* work:

- To be the best startup community in the world, region, state
- To foster a better startup community than a peer city
- To create X number of unicorns in my region

6   Linda Hill and Kent Lineback, "The Fundamental Purpose of Your Team," *Harvard Business Review*, July 12, 2011, https://hbr.org/2011/07/the-fundamental-purpose-of-you.html.

- To fix our economy

Warning: [Insert rant here.] My least-favorite purpose is to set a goal to be better than another city. Startup community building cannot be a competition. This goal will cloud your activities and will never get you or your community on the right trajectory. This purpose might help you rally the troops and might help you secure some funding (what politician doesn't like to create the drama of an identifiable foe?), but this purpose is short-lived, as it inherently creates activities that don't move the community forward. I can't make it through a day without seeing some new list that ranks the best communities. Don't get caught up in this trap—being "better" than your peer city cannot be your purpose. There's really only one core to your purpose: helping entrepreneurs become more successful.

Another reason why the above purposes don't work is that they're narrowly focused on the end result. They assume an ability to engineer an outcome. (Reminder, if it were possible to engineer an outcome, then we'd have Silicon Valleys all around the world.) This feels overly linear, with an implied focus on what needs to be managed. This makes many people feel more comfortable, but it ultimately creates a false sense of purpose.

Here are a few startup community purposes I like better:

- To create great activities that support new founders and engage the whole community
- To publicly share an outline and a clear path forward for anyone dreaming of starting a company
- To connect everyone interested in playing a role in our startup community

- To help every entrepreneur, regardless of where they are in their startup journey
- To create a diverse community by adding teenagers, retirees, and everyone in between
- To see traditional and social media showcase the journey of hardworking founders
- To attend a startup meetup X times per month

Do you see that my examples are more tangible? Do you see that my examples are more compelling and that they drive a clearer set of actions that I and others can easily engage and support?

Momentum is every startup community's best friend. One of the key reasons behind taking a short-term complexity mindset or taking a short-term collective purpose to your community-building activities is that a series of small, quick wins builds momentum. And momentum is contagious. Invariably, you'll seek some sponsorship, grant, or investment dollars to accelerate your mission. The bottom line is, the institutions that provide those dollars want to see that what you're doing works. Take too big of a swing that's more conceptual than actual, and you put those future dollars at risk. I would also add that every investment dollar provided is done so with risk. Your task is to mitigate as much of that risk as possible. One way to do that is to create simpler activities with simpler measurement tools and outcomes. Combine this with leaders whose credibility matches the tasks at hand, and you have a winning formula.

PRINCIPLE #5: BUILD THE FORT

I led this chapter in the original *Build the Fort* book with the statement, "Every journey begins with the first step." It remains a slightly cheesy cliché today as it did back then, but we have already embraced my cheesy build-the-fort metaphor. So let's run it to the end, shall we?

My thought partner and friend Brad Feld shared that a startup community–building effort is a twenty-year journey. I modified his thought with the notion that this is a generational change we are undertaking. Generational changes have many parents and startup community building is no exception. Many parents in this context means many actors, many leaders, many ideas, many activities, many companies, and many failures.

I cannot tell you exactly what your community needs to speed forward. I can tell you that a methodology of many little bets that works for startups can work for startup community building.[7] Our thesis on effective community building is a riff on a well-known cliche: "Success will be through a thousand nudges."

There is only one principle or a hint of wisdom that I can share from my observations and experiences—you just have to start and start with a nudge.

The world is littered with new ideas that never see the light of day.

The world is littered with good intentions never put into action.

It's easy for one to see Silicon Valley or Hyderabad or Berlin as these magical entrepreneurial mountains that can never be mimicked. But these places are not your goal, and your collec-

---

7   http://petersims.com/little-bets/.

tive steps to optimize your city shouldn't be dependent on their journeys.

The fort metaphor works if you let it. My fort building exuded a combination of urgency (let's see what we can do over the next several days) and patience (we aren't building the Taj Mahal, so let's do the best we can with what we have).

Like a startup founder, community builders need to operate with no inhibition. It's not easy for leaders who are assigned this task to report their findings to a boss or board. Fear gets in the way of innovation. Just ask any successful entrepreneur. Community leaders need to adopt that same emotion.

The corollary to inhibition is permission. More specifically, the desire or need to ask permission to act. As shared before, there is no CEO or one leader of the ecosystem. So why seek permission? It only creates an unhelpful working dynamic. In Principle #2 I used the term *peer*. Operate as an equal. You don't need permission from anyone to take positive action in your community!

Just be courteous while not kissing the ring of some perceived leader. Hopefully over time you can get them to buy into your new mindset.

Be inclusive of all actors, but don't blindly follow the wrong leaders.

Smile and bring a positive vibe to all interactions, but get shit done.

Also, have fun and don't take this too seriously. There are no exact right answers or outcomes, and we're all just experimenting anyway. The following chart (meant to be read left to right for every bullet) frames your dichotomous mindset and approach.

Complicated VS Complex Leadership

Old Way	New Way
• Top Down	• Grass Roots
• Government Led	• Entrepreneur Led
• Hierarchical Structure	• Network Structure
• Command & Control	• Self-Organized
• Design Strategic Plan	• Experiments / Iterations

As I mentioned, ultimate community success is through a thousand nudges. Be a community-building entrepreneur and take the leap: act on the first nudge that you are most motivated to do. Find a handful of fellow enthusiasts who also think like ten-year-old fort builders and ask them to help you with that nudge. Then turn around and help them with theirs. Utilize your new relationships to analyze where the community is today and where you all want it to go tomorrow. Create a bias for action among a team of five to eight, including a few entrepreneurs, and focus on collaboration, support, and inclusivity. Do it and don't look back.

FRAMEWORK

THE COMPONENTS OF STARTUP COMMUNITY BUILDING

I love maps. Maybe that's why I am a cartographer with an undergraduate and master's degree in geography. I learned how to write software in college in 1979–1981. Those two things are a good source for my leading role in the MapQuest journey. The reason I share this backstory is because I love the concept of a roadmap. Go back to when you were a kid. Do you have memories of staring at a Rand McNally Road Atlas on a family road trip? Needless to say, I do. The very ideas of charting our driving path, looking for what's around us, and the natural feeling of comfort from knowing where we are going are all derived from the roadmap.

We tend to look for roadmaps in other parts of our lives too, and building out our local startup community is no exception. For some, the term *roadmap* can be thought of as a plan or strategy intended to achieve a particular goal.[8] In this section, I will outline a simple roadmap for you and your community, complete with plenty of ideas and concepts that wrap around our counterintuitive framework.

But first, what is a framework? Here are three ideas:

1. "A basic structure underlying a system, concept, or text."[9]
2. "A real or conceptual structure intended to serve as a support or guide for the building of something that expands the structure into something useful."[10]

8   Dictionary.com, s.v. "roadmap," accessed February 13, 2023, https://www.lexico.com/definition/road_map.

9   Oxford Languages, s.v. "framework," accessed February 13, 2023, https://www.google.com/search?q=dictionary+framework&oq=dictionary+framework.

10 Ben Lutkevich, "framework," WhatIs.com, last modified August 2020, https://www.techtarget.com/whatis/definition/framework.

3. "A particular set of rules, ideas, or beliefs which you use in order to deal with problems or to decide what to do."[11]

THREE FRAMEWORKS

Over the course of this book, I will outline three ways to both simplify and visualize elements of our complexity mindset:

1. An Asset Framework
2. A Community Maturity Framework
3. A Development and Engagement Framework

These are in order. They leverage the *Build the Fort* mindset and principles.

This is what I do.

I simplify the complex so that others can better understand and then act on that understanding. Bear with me if these seem to be overlapping or repetitive.

---

11 *Collins Dictionary*, s.v. "framework," accessed February 13, 2023, https://www.collinsdictionary.com/us/dictionary/english/framework.

CHAPTER 3

ASSET FRAMEWORK

Our high-level asset framework organizes around three distinct building blocks that every startup community needs. I call them the startup community Activities, Actors, and Attitudes.

This is a very simple framework for sharing with complicated thinkers what you are up to by introducing the idea of "attitudes" into the mix. By introducing attitudes as a key driver, we begin to subtly move away from the engineered, activities-only mindset.

These building blocks are best represented in the following chart:

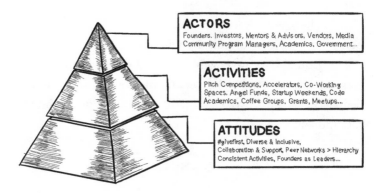

ACTORS
Founders, Investors, Mentors & Advisors, Vendors, Media
Community Program Managers, Academics, Government...

ACTIVITIES
Pitch Competitions, Accelerators, Co-Working
Spaces, Angel Funds, Startup Weekends, Code
Academics, Coffee Groups, Grants, Meetups...

ATTITUDES
#givefirst, Diverse & Inclusive,
Collaboration & Support, Peer Networks > Hierarchy
Consistent Activities, Founders as Leaders...

The best sources for this inventory are the people you've been meeting with. They not only provide you information about the activities, but they also give off some important signals. For example, if you keep hearing about the same event from everyone, then I would surmise that it's working well (or well enough). If you hear about an event but nobody ever mentions it, that's also a (more negative) signal.

ACTORS

In my work at Techstars (and now as a solo consultant), I created a simple assessment spreadsheet with a list of important actors across the major actor categories, including

- founders;
- investors;
- serial founders;
- university instructors, researchers, program managers;
- corporate innovation leaders;
- government and non-government leaders;
- community leaders (entrepreneurial support organizations);
- media (traditional and non-traditional); and
- real estate (coworking space managers).

Please take a 360-degree view of this activity. Getting a broad perspective on the community will only serve you better in the long run. When we began our initial engagements with a community, we would typically talk to anywhere from 75 to 150 people across the ecosystem. This may seem daunting, but it's totally doable.

In fall of 2009 and the following spring, I was enthusiastic about creating a Techstars-inspired accelerator in Raleigh-Durham. Brad Feld of Foundry Group and David Cohen of Techstars were two of the first people I connected with. David advised me on accelerator practices, and Brad mentored me on community building. I proceeded to have a coffee, lunch, or end-of-day frosty beverage with about 275 people in six months. I can assure you that I uncovered a boatload of information about what was going on and what was not. As importantly, I built strong connections with a number of these 275 initial contacts, many of whom are now close friends and fellow community builders.

Fast-forward to today, and though I don't have a definitive number, I am confident that I've met one-on-one with at least three thousand local contacts over the past decade. I share this with you to set a bar of what can be done if it's important to you. Today I call this initial work my gold. Not bad for a guy who doesn't drink coffee. :-)

Here are some web searches that will help you identify the actors in the ecosystem:

- **Google**
  - Your city + startup community
  - Your city + crunchbase
  - Your city + angellist
  - "Founder" search on LinkedIn + your city
- **Meetup:** The key here is to look at events and write down the names of people who are either running or attending them. Basic search terms for finding events:
  - Founder
  - Entrepreneur
  - Startup

- Software development
- Technology (Java, Python, React)

One of the characteristics of a nascent, developing, and even emerging ecosystem is that no one has a definitive map of all of the actors. So go build your own and then share it with everyone.

An easy place to start when inventorying actors and their activities is to just ask everyone where the founders hang out. This is akin to the old adage coined by the famous criminal Willie Sutton, when asked why he robbed banks. His response was, "Because that's where the money is." Following the founders is my best advice to determine what is and what is not happening in your community.

While collecting this information there are a number of ways to codify your work. Many use a simple spreadsheet. I use some mind-mapping tools (MindManager is my fave) as I'm a visual person. A whiteboard or a couple of large sticky pages will do. There will be lots of information to visualize. Regardless, it is imperative that you capture the information when you are getting started because after a few weeks, contacts and crumbs of information begin to fade from memory.

ACTIVITIES

While you're searching for people, you will invariably come across a number of community activities. To be clear, I use the word *activity* in its broadest definition within this framework. An activity is anything that serves the entrepreneur along their journey.

Activities come in all shapes and sizes, but there are some more common ones:

- Networking (coffee, beer/wine/soda)
- Inspire new founders (my Idea2Launch workshop, finding a co-founder, Startup Weekend)
- Growth founder/CEO get-togethers (informal dinners, etc.)
- Investment pitches (pitch competitions)
- Functional skill development (marketing, software development, mental health, hiring/firing, etc.)
- Grant programs, accelerators, incubators (they are different), venture funds
- Coworking spaces primarily focused on entrepreneurs
- General support (Startup Grind, Founders Institute, etc.)

As outlined above, there are also easy web searches that can help you map the ecosystem activities. To repeat:

- **Google**
  - Your city + "startup community"
  - Your city + "seed investment"
  - Your city + "business mentorship"
- **Meetup:** The key here is to find events or meetup sites that address founders and their journey from idea to exit. Basic search terms:
  - Founder
  - Entrepreneur
  - Startup
  - Software development
  - Technology (Java, Python, React)

A critical element of the event audit is to understand the breadth, quality, quantity, and frequency of each activity. These are all pretty important. Why? You are trying to determine what's working and what isn't. You're trying to find gaps to fill or new formats to change the event mojo. Onward and upward, right?

The best way to evaluate an activity is to show up. Then find the activity leaders. Then ask them to grab a coffee and get the history of how this activity got to this place and time. Or write down the common activities while meeting the actors. More importantly, start to understand who leads these activities (these are the existing "influencers" and they are very important today and may be tomorrow).

A few things I would find out about each activity:

- Who shows up? Both categorically and individually.
- How many show up? Is it consistent?
- How do people find out about the event? Are there newbies every time? Do they come back (are they welcomed)?
- Does the format change?
- How often is the event held? Is that frequency consistent? For how long has this event been held?
- Why did you start/host the event?
- What motivates you to volunteer your time to this event?
- Do you see any activity gaps that aren't being addressed, and if so, why don't we have someone leading that activity?

Activity breadth, quality, quantity, and frequency collectively signal a certain state or maturity of the community. More does not guarantee better (forgetting quality and frequency).

Hopefully this all makes sense and you understand the value in building connections, credibility, and knowledge. But that's not all. There's something much deeper you need to inventory—attitudes.

ATTITUDES

Each community and its individual members carry with them both an individual attitude and a collective attitude about the community. As attitudes are the foundation of a great community, it's critical to understand them along with the activity inventory.

I've seen the results of good attitudes versus unhealthy ones when applied to a startup community. It's a real thing and it matters a whole lot. But before we go on, I want to review what we've agreed to so far:

1. Founders are the center of all activity. Non-entrepreneurs serve entrepreneurs.
2. Communities are inclusive of anyone who wants to play a role.
3. No one owns the community. There is no CEO.
4. The community mission comes before one's own needs.

With these in mind, what are some of the attitudes we are looking for from individual members of our community:

- Supportive or selfish?
- Entrepreneur-led or organization-led?
- Givefirst or transactional?
- Network or hierarchical?

- Inclusive (tribal) or clustered silos?
- Vote with their feet or just with their mouths?

I bet you can determine someone's attitude within the first fifteen minutes of meeting them. Your job is to find people who are already exhibiting the right attitude. Your second task is to recruit some of the wrong-thinkers over to the right-thinkers by educating them through books (this one is a great start, as well as Brad's first *Startup Community* book), one-on-one sessions, and perseverance. More on that later.

I know that some of you (the engineering types or complicated thinkers) are wondering how you can build a more efficient process for this audit/inventory. Though I applaud your motivation to go faster, I must warn you that you'll miss a great deal of nuance around the attitudes if you stress speed. Not many great relationships are built with speed as the overriding factor.

Individual interviews yield high-quality information. I strongly recommend this approach. In-person connections will serve as a seed for future work, trust, and credibility—machines aren't good at that, at least not yet.

Surveys are a wonderful tool to gather lots of information. But there's a good chance the data won't be very valuable, at least in terms of evaluating attitudes. When it comes to how people feel about something that's important to them, a common finding is that they adjust their answers under pressure. Some may be motivated to act more like cheerleaders for the community, and others may have an ax to grind with one or more of the local support organizations—and they use the survey to share their displeasure.

At the end of the day, there's nothing like having a face-to-face conversation with your community peers. At best, a survey can augment that work, but not replace it. A survey is a proxy for attitudes, but if you really want to understand and gauge the people in your community, you're going to have to interact with them: talk to them, listen to them, work with them, and, yes, disagree and struggle with them.

Segue with me here. I love data. There's a feeling of comfort that it provides, especially when you're faced with a difficult decision. I advise startup founders to find ways to create data-driven decisions. For startup community enthusiasts and those of you with that complicated mindset, you're going to want some data to support your visions.

I'm right there with you. But like many things, there's a right way and a wrong way to do data. Let's start with the wrong way.

As much as I love data, I hate Top Whatever lists. You know what I'm referring to. "The Top 10 Cities for Startups," or "These Are Your 2022 Fastest Growing Startup Cities." They're clickbait at best, and at worst they cloud an already difficult challenge.

These lists are trailing indicators of activity. Which means there is no signal or clue as to what you should do more or less to drive future progress. At worst, community builders use these lists to somehow generically copy the activities of the city ranked ahead of them, thinking that doing so will yield the same results. Let me ask you this one simple question: what should you do differently tomorrow based on where your city is ranked in any of these lists? The answer is *nothing*. That's why these lists are all but useless.

Remember one of my truths: Startup communities are like children. They should never be compared.

What works for one community has little bearing on what will work for yours. In Durham, we love nighttime events. In Louisville, Kentucky, they like morning events.

These lists aren't data. They're vanity metrics. Not only are they not actionable, but they also set a tone and attitude that are counter to what your community needs. Startup communities require leaders who are focused on how to be the best community possible, not how to be better than some peer city that has a completely different set of assets, leaders, and organizations, as well as its own distinct culture. Ignore the lists and don't play into the trap they encourage.

Want to collect some actionable data? Analyze the information on attendees at various events and track it over time. Look for the number of new attendees (which supports more connectivity), and measure your diversity efforts by noting their demographics. These are both better indicators of long-term change in your community.

There is some cross-community analysis that can be helpful to community builders. A few examples are *Inc. Magazine*'s "Surge Cities," Richard Florida's "Creative Class Cities," and Ian Hathaway and Florida's *Rise of the Global Startup City* report.[12] We naturally will look at other cities to see what they are doing and compare ourselves to them. Look, analyze, then experiment, but don't compare.

---

12   https://www.inc.com/surge-cities; https://www.citylab.com/life/2015/04/americas-leading-creative-class-cities-in-2015/390852/; http://startupsusa.org/global-startup-cities/.

As part of a shared understanding of both your community and other communities, it is smart to see what others are doing to move their community forward. Like a startup or any other entity-building activity, we never have enough good information, so look to others for inspiration and best practices.

CHAPTER 4

ECOSYSTEM MATURITY FRAMEWORK

So far, you've bought into the Build the Fort mindset. You went out and performed an audit or inventory of the people, the activities, and the attitudes of your ecosystem. You met great people. You attended many different events. And now you have some ideas of how people connect, collaborate, and support one another.

It is helpful then to gather all of this information and organize it into another framework. Our next task is to determine where the community/ecosystem is in terms of its life cycle.

My belief is that by really understanding where the region is, we can then prioritize the types of activities needed to push us to the next level. I have found that too many communities are optimizing for activities that the community is not mature enough to take advantage of as yet.

STAGES OF ECOSYSTEM MATURITY

I look at startup communities as being in one of four stages of maturity:

1. Nascent
2. Developing
3. Emerging
4. Leading

We categorize a startup community in one of these stages not to compare the community with others, but so that we can focus on activities that are appropriate for the stage a community is in. This is why an honest ecosystem audit is so important.

A very real example is finding the appropriate stage for a $100 million venture fund. That investment is best applied at the leading or possibly emerging stages, but never the developing or nascent stages. Why? Because good money thrown at immature ideas (or immature founders) is wasted money. Of course you won't know that for another few years, when the cash runs out. After the five-year mark, maybe a few of the millions-deployed-at-the-wrong-stage companies went on to raise more money (an important signal) or, more importantly, they developed some growth traction. "The $100 million fund announcement was special, though! The politicians showed up. The ribbon-cutting-like atmosphere was exciting too!" But where were the entrepreneurs? At best they were in the back row for the photo op. At worst, your community has lost credibility with local investment professionals for years to come.

Not only have this effort and money been wasted, but this now creates a very real signal that this ecosystem cannot build breakout companies. Those funders walk away with that unfortunate idea, and you've now moved your ecosystem backward, not forward.

Yet, the miracle local venture fund (usually funded by the government) is one of the first go-to activities of uninformed ecosystem champions. Their intentions are pure, but their knowledge and mindset are imperfect.

There is a set of activities and a focus that are more appropriate for the ecosystem at each stage of maturity. Through our global reach and experience, we have an understanding of which activities will activate your community and which ones you need to defer a few years.

In this way, you—as one of the ecosystem leaders—can look at peer communities and see which activities seem to be creating the engagement you need.

NASCENT STAGE

One dictionary definition of nascent is "just coming into existence and beginning to display signs of future potential."[13] The Latin origin is "being born."

The majority of cities in the world are at the nascent stage of growing their startup communities. I've visited over seventy-five cities in the last five years. I've met with ecosystem actors from

---

13   Oxford Languages, s.v. "nascent," accessed February 13, 2023, https://www.google.com/
    search?q=nascent&rlz=1C5CHFA_enUS1000US1000&oq=
    nasce&aqs=chrome.o.69i59l3j69i57j46i175i199i512j69i60j69i61j69i60.2404j1j9&sourceid=
    chrome&ie=UTF-8.

all walks of life. I share this with you so that I can honestly level set the reality of your ecosystem's stage and the mountain left for you to climb.

Most of your cities are just coming into existence regardless of how long you've had those handful of entrepreneurial programs. You have programs that are in place. These are good signals. The existence of your entrepreneurial support organizations and their programs are not really related to the future outcomes you desire, are they?

At the nascent stage of your community, you're still very much in experiment mode. Leaders are emerging, but they have no startup community–building experience. Most have never lived in a community that's in a further stage (emerging or leading). That's okay. From my point of view, this just means you have less baggage and less history to work through. It is the proverbial blank sheet of paper.

Founders may be few, but several of them have been at it for a long time. These individuals are often the de facto leaders of the community. The relative set of experiences that founders have in more mature communities don't exist in your nascent community. Said another way, the founders don't know what they don't know.

Angel investors are nonexistent as well. There is no collaboration with the local colleges or universities, and mentorship, if available, is programmatically sparse and performed by former businesspeople, not other founders. Local corporations have no interactions with startups or investment groups and are likely not even aware of the regional activities.

Example cities in this stage I've worked in include Columbia, South Carolina; Fort Wayne, Indiana; and Louisville, Kentucky.

DEVELOPING STAGE

At this stage of your startup community, the programs, activities, and events are being stood up and there are obvious outcomes from some of those activities. New founders are emerging. Local angel investors are making a handful of small, one-time investments. There are one or more mentor programs available to founders. And there are some consistent (weekly or monthly) activities that interested actors engage in.

At the very least, the number of net new founders is growing, and that is seen and felt by everyone—they aren't behind closed doors. Though there might be activity gaps in the overall community, the existing activities are well attended, which means they provide obvious value to the attendees. These events might even be growing in attendance. Another great signal that you are at a developing stage as an ecosystem is that the news of key startup company inflection points is easily known by enthusiasts in the community. Whether it's a community blog, the local newspaper, posts on LinkedIn and Twitter, or just a healthy dose of old-fashioned one-on-one networking meetings where news is shared, people know that companies are "winning."

Local corporations are still very removed from the startup community though there may be conversations starting that begin to find ways to integrate into the ecosystem. Experienced executives are starting to connect with breakout founders and their companies.

College or university collaboration isn't happening. Many of these institutions have entrepreneur classes, but there is no discernible integration with the private sector for mentorship or support.

Government leaders have discussions and even some financial support for the ecosystem, but those activities aren't moving the needle very far. And if those programs are fully funded and supported, the government leaders are taking an oversized role in dictating the rules of engagement.

Example cities in the developing stage I have worked in include Cleveland, Ohio; Buffalo, New York; and Birmingham, Alabama.

EMERGING STAGE

Communities at an emerging stage have developed a foundation focused on founders, mentorship, and leadership over multiple years. The community-building progress is obvious even to newcomers and those typically on the periphery. Multiple leaders begin to take on a broader set of activities to build, leverage, and sustain progress.

Growth can be measured by numbers, sentiment, and community-wide participants.

You can count the founders in the hundreds, as an example. More founders translates into more investors. More investors morph into syndicated investments. Even out-of-town, regional venture capitalists are starting to show up and make an investment or two.

At this stage, your community has multiple entities (ESOs, or entrepreneurial service organizations). Local corporations are getting involved in meaningful ways. Perhaps their executives are mentoring emerging leaders, even encouraging employees with ideas to become intrapreneurs—or, better yet, entrepreneurs.

The ties to the colleges and universities are becoming more integrated. The overall ecosystem is widening, with more observers connecting and trying to figure out what roles they can play (or what's in it for them).

One of the truest signals is the in-migration of existing startups to the area. The word is out! A-grade founders are moving to the area from smaller, regional cities as they see that they can find resources that are not available in their current locales. The same for executive talent from larger Tier 1 cities. They went to college here, or their spouse's family is here, and they are starting to have children and want a different lifestyle for their family than they find in New York City, Los Angeles, or Dallas.

Example cities in the emerging stage I've worked in include Raleigh-Durham, North Carolina; Taipei, Taiwan; and Des Moines, Iowa.

LEADING STAGE

As a leading ecosystem, you have a wide and deep set of activities across all aspects of entrepreneurship. Governments are supporting and many times creating support programs. Colleges and universities have advanced entrepreneur curriculums, but students are starting real companies while in school. Scientists and researchers are seeing regular commercialization of their work.

Corporations serve as investors, workforce development partners, acquirers, customers, and distribution partners at every stage of a startup company's life cycle.

New founders are dropping out of their jobs at existing corporations and are supported in that decision. Founders represent a cross section of their city in terms of diversity (gender, race, age, educational attainment, etc.). The new founders are embraced and supported with programming that meets their needs where they sit today (as opposed to forcing them through another entrepreneurial door or window).

Mentorship comes in a variety of ways and seems to happen seamlessly, with no organizational effort. Though there are group programs, true mentorship comes in the ad hoc, one-on-one meetings that peer founders create every day.

Investments emerge from a large cross section of investors, including grants from the government, alumni venture funds from the local college, individual angels, and angel groups (which include local successful entrepreneurs). Locally focused venture funds as well as a continual stream of outside venture firms make frequent visits to your city.

Getting an idea of where your ecosystem maturity lies with an honest appraisal based on data, anecdotes, interview notes, etc., provides leaders with a framework to now decide what to do first and what to kick down the road.

Example cities I've spent time in that were in this stage include Austin, Texas; Seattle, Washington; and Berlin, Germany.

CHAPTER 5

ENGAGEMENT FRAMEWORK

In parallel to the four stages of ecosystem maturity, we identified seven basic cornerstone drivers of activity with respect to your startup community and entrepreneurial ecosystem activities:

1. **Develop Leaders:** Setting the Right Attitudes among Current and New Local Leaders
2. **Develop Founders:** Inspiring and Supporting Founders
3. **Develop Mentors:** Increasing the Current Level of Mentorship for Founders at All Stages
4. **Develop Investors:** Activating More Local and Regional Investors
5. **Engage Corporations:** Connecting Regional Corporations into the Ecosystem
6. **Engage Universities:** Connecting Regional Universities/Colleges into the Ecosystem
7. **Engage Government:** Securing Support with Local, Regional, State, and Federal Government in Support of the Ecosystem.

So far, we've outlined why we are motivated to build a more

robust startup community and ecosystem. We've also shared a few frameworks to set the viewpoint we should take to understand where we are and what's important.

Now we're going to focus on the how—the meat of this book and the information you've all been waiting for. So, we developed an engagement framework.

Our framework has seven drivers. This is what makes sense to me in my pursuit of simplifying the complex. Go on this road trip with me a little further and let's not ponder about who made the atlas and whether the roads should be black or gray.

DRIVER #1: DEVELOP LEADERS

The first and most foundational of the seven drivers of startup community and entrepreneurial ecosystem building is leadership. Leadership means so many different things to different people. Throughout this book, I've offered a mindset, an attitude, maybe even a framework or three that you could deploy in your ecosystem. When you break down the intent of this book to its core purpose, it's to make *you* a great leader. Why?

My experience is this: if you can adopt the principles outlined here and then be armed with a new or augmented set of tactics, and then prioritize connecting with members of your ecosystem, your future work will ultimately invite a new set of community norms. How?

It turns out that we influence our friends and our friends' friends and even our friends' friends' friends without even being intentional about our influence.

What if we were actually intentional about sharing those new principles? Like every hour of every day of every week? Imagine the influence we could create. What if we found a handful of peers to do the same thing?

At Techstars we talked a lot about the culture of a community. Culture is the collective bucket of the current community norms. We also developed tools, tricks, and programs around setting a new community culture. If that sounds like an impossible task, you're not alone in thinking so. But what if we only needed to change eight or ten people and then had the patience for that invisible influence to diffuse throughout the community?

That is ecosystem leadership.

In their excellent book *Connected,* Nicholas Christakis and James Fowler explain the amazing power of social networks and our profound influence on one another's lives.[14] The premise of their research shows that if we affect our friends, and they affect their friends, then our actions can potentially affect people we have never met. This is a radical and extreme concept for developing a new startup community culture based on the principles outlined in this book.

For both new and existing startup community leaders who are seeking ways to change, it takes a monumental task (changing the actions and behaviors of hundreds of community members) and requires one to focus their efforts on just a handful of leaders. If you can take that effort and intentionally target the local influencers, you might just be able to accelerate cultural change.

---

14   Nicholas A. Christakis and James H. Fowler, *Connected: The Surprising Power of Our Social Networks and How They Shape Our Lives* (New York: Little, Brown and Company, 2009).

As the writers summarize so perfectly, "Social networks, it turns out, tend to amplify whatever they are seeded with."

Throughout this book, I've shared ideas from *Startup Communities*, *The Startup Community Way*, and *Build the Fort: Why 5 Simple Lessons You Learned as a 10-Year-Old Can Set You Up for Startup Success*, and many of my thoughts from my writing for Inc.com and my personal blog. Our goal is to collectively share the same mindset, but what follows mindset? The following is a list of the ecosystem norms that everyone must adopt and pledge to uphold:

1. To serve the ecosystem, my company, and myself.
2. To contribute to the growth of this ecosystem (because I know it will benefit everyone, not just me).
3. To welcome and embrace everyone into our ecosystem.
4. To create an inclusive and welcoming environment for all participants.
5. To support underrepresented individuals and groups in their pursuit of entrepreneurship and proactively reach out to them for inclusion in this community.
6. To operate in the spirit of collaboration, and avoid competition, even though I might come out ahead if I were to compete.
7. To connect individuals asking for help from my network when possible with as little curation or filters as reasonable.
8. To reject the idea of gatekeepers and ensure everyone in the community is treated as an equal with equal access to information and resources.
9. To put founders first, which means making decisions based on what would be best for a founder and their company.
10. To #givefirst whenever possible, without expecting anything

in return. I will take meetings when asked and offer advice without payment.

11. To operate in an honorable manner by doing what I said I would do.

12. To publicly exhibit my love of this place (your city) in all interactions (face-to-face, social media, etc.).

13. To exhibit daily a spirit of Win-Win, not a Zero-Sum or Win-Lose mentality.

14. To foster the next generation of entrepreneurs and ecosystem leaders.

15. To publicly support this pledge as often as possible, and encourage others in the ecosystem to do so as well.

THE PLEDGE

Do you agree with the above? More so, do you fully embrace these principles? If you want to change your ecosystem and serve as an ecosystem influencer, you not only have to believe, but you must publicly recognize these principles and put them into action.

One simple way you and/or your peers can exhibit influence is to publicly commit to these principles. Think of it like the no-drinking pledge that high school seniors make before prom. As part of our ecosystem development work, we might stand up a site containing the pledge so anyone can review and personally commit to it.

AN INFLUENCER CIRCLE

This is a fancy name for a mutual support group. Our version of this concept is to identify and recruit around ten individuals in the community who are in positions of leadership or influence (remember that these can be different people—not all leaders are influencers, and not all influencers have formal roles as leaders).

We curate and invite these people from the community to join our influencer circle with the mission of breaking down formal organizational walls, mutually acknowledge the challenges in the community and ecosystem, and share a willingness to put their personal or business agendas to the side and sign up for the greater mission of the community.

Our concept of an influencer circle does not involve creating a name for the group (or a website) and we are definitely not appointing any officers. Those elements have the notion of a different motivation from the one we're after. This is not for position, for your resume, or to build individual power and control.

Here is a list of principles inspired and adapted from others on how to run an influencer circle:

- The group should have a common understanding of the mission of the startup community.
- Determine a shared mission and goals that need to be achieved.
- There is no designated leader, though someone can play meeting facilitator.
- The group operates with mutual respect for one another and respects each other's thoughts, ideas, and challenges.
- Each member commits to operating in an honest and transparent manner.
- The group meets regularly (such as monthly).

- Focus discussion on ourselves, not on others in or outside the group.
- Remind each other of the mission, goals, and pledge principles that this group is trying to foster throughout the ecosystem.
- Keep track of your group's progress.
- Share responsibility for the group.
- Be sure everyone has a chance to talk.
- Emphasize the importance of confidentiality.
- Encourage outside contact among members.
- Share rewards and failures.
- Keep a realistic perspective.[15]

The hardest part is the first few meetings. Individually, everyone understands why they chose to be part of the group. Collectively, though, you haven't found the common mission and how this group will rally around it. Many times the place to start is by agreeing with the challenges or impediments to progress that everyone is feeling.

A version of this type of meeting is called a charrette. From the World Bank: "A charrette is a type of participatory planning process that assembles an interdisciplinary team—typically consisting of planners, citizens, city officials, architects, landscape architects, transportation engineers, parks and recreation officials, and other stakeholders—to create a design and implementation plan for a specific project."[16] A key component of the charrette is time compression.

---

15   Lisa Kramarchyk, "Guidelines for Effective Group Work" (Psyc 220, SUNY Oneonta, New York, October 2003), http://employees.oneonta.edu/vomsaaw/w/psy220/files/GroupWorkGuidelines.htm.

16   "Charettes," The World Bank, accessed February 23, 2023, https://urban-regeneration.worldbank.org/node/40.

The process of making a good charrette is summarized as follows:

- Charette participants work collaboratively.
- The team designs cross-functionally.
- Charrettes use design to achieve a shared vision and create holistic solutions.
- Designers work on the big picture and the details.
- A tight time frame for the work schedule facilitates resolution.
- The team communicates in short feedback loops.
- The charette lasts between four and seven days.
- It's held on-site.
- The charette results in a buildable plan.

Our Influencer Circles use the spirit of a charrette while developing deeper relationships that orient around a shared common mission. One of the ah-ha moments in every group meeting is the lack of a common view of the challenge. Most leaders only see the problem through their own organization's lens. This is limiting to say the least, and problematic to collaboration.

AMPLIFY YOUR VOICE

The underlying goal is for you and your peers to embrace the ecosystem principles and proactively share and support them throughout your community. If this sounds daunting, you may be overthinking the goal. Just do your thing. I hereby deputize you as an agent of change. Show up at events. Guest speak at college classes, judge competitions, and sit on panels.

OPEN OFFICE HOURS

Every interaction you have creates an opportunity to support the new norms of this ecosystem. This is one of the easiest ways to interact with the community. But as a current or emerging leader, you must put yourself out there. There's no reason not to meet with three to five people every week. Do the math. The gross number of interactions in this vehicle can easily get to a hundred over the course of a year. To be clear, in 2009–2010, when I wanted to meet everyone in and around the Raleigh-Durham ecosystem, I had over 275 meetings in five months and probably over a thousand in the next twelve to fifteen months. Granted, I had the time, and I allocated four days a week for most of the first five months solely to this task.

Make the office hours public. Host them at the coworking spaces that house the most founders. Ask them to put your calendar in their marketing materials. Ask other founders (met from your tour) to join you for a couple of hours a week. Be available!

LOCAL COFFEES, MEETUPS, PANELS, CONFERENCES

These are happening every day around your town. This is a classic one-to-many opportunity. In most cases, when asked to "say a few words," you get the floor. Why not take the opportunity to make aware, educate, and support through your actions any one of these principles? People will react stronger when they see that your actions support their words.

The operative thought here is "show up." And given recent events, this can be both in person or virtually through video chats. You can't believe the impact you can have as a community leader when you show up at other people's events.

In fall of 2016, I found myself in Brad's office talking about the evolution of startup communities. In particular, I was wondering about a low level of tension between two of my communities, Raleigh and Durham, which are separated by twenty-five miles or so. Brad calls these "binary stars," and I recognized that there was a parallel between Denver and Boulder—one that exists on many ironic planes.

Brad shared that they had gone through a lot of the same tensions, friction, finger-pointing, and basic behavioral outbursts. (Feels like sibling rivalry, right?) I asked how it has evolved and he answered in a very simple way.

If you want to fix it, you have to publicly and consistently do one thing—show up. Support them and their events by showing up and then ask them to do the same. Do it often and do it so everyone can see your behavior. Over time, this tension will heal itself.

There are other ways you can support these coffee meetups, panels, AMAs (ask me anything), and conferences. You can share your gold.

What gold do you have? You have a contact list. Now, I realize that some of those people you met once and exchanged cards. In some cases, though, even that level of depth is enough to get them to show up at your friends' events. And many times your email to them with all of your leadership mojo can be enough to take the attendee list from twenty-five to fifty. This is significant. The energy of a room with twenty-five versus fifty people is palpable. And now that event has fifty evangelists working to make it seventy-five. This is a positive contagion, and your outbound email support had something to do with accelerating that activity.

You can also just fill a gap with your own idea. A few years into the Raleigh-Durham startup community renaissance, after I had met one-on-one with at least a thousand local community members, I started to see this email show up in my inbox: "Hey, Chris. I know you know people—I'm looking for a salesperson, software developer, finance freelancer, etc." I would respond to every one of them with two to three names. No double opt-in here—just good old-fashioned Joe meet Mary, Mary meet Joe.

After a while I started to wonder why this simple networking concept wasn't being addressed through traditional means like job fairs, recruiters, or job boards. I then thought about my hiring experiences as a founder/CEO and realized that those vehicles are not run for early-stage companies. Early-stage companies need something new, something different, something unique just for them.

A few months later the Big Top was born. It was an event set in a circus-themed environment where the startup founders pitched the audience on why they should come work for their company (this reverses the selling proposition). This event took into account that these connections were going to be different.

After five years, dozens of events, and the hiring of hundreds of people, I ran out of time and energy and sold the side hustle business to a local group. The point here is that I saw a need, I had some fun by figuring out a unique way to address the need, I socialized the idea and found a few partners and figured it out from there.

BLOGS, TWITTER, FACEBOOK, AND INSTAGRAM...

Yes, I too am overwhelmed with this list, as well as the platforms that come and go and the ones yet to be important. But they're all vehicles you can use to elevate your voice. These platforms are all about sharing your principles and displaying your leadership skills. It's incumbent upon you to exhibit your support for the principles outlined previously. It's up to you to decide which platforms to use, but you need to be on one or more, and you have to consistently share your thoughts.

Each platform has a different rhythm and tone, and while you may find the same people across multiple platforms, each product offers a unique experience that audiences have come to expect. Think of it as your opportunity to target these audiences with some community messaging. I just gave you a template for the principles, and there are probably three or four mini thoughts within each of them. Your task is to keep your eyes and ears open for either good or bad observations, and share your thoughts on them.

LinkedIn is great with a short post (fifty to one hundred words) and a good picture.

Twitter is for short bursts and is best for daily drops.

A blog should have at least a weekly posting cadence to be effective.

Facebook can be a repost from your blog or a picture and a few lines.

Instagram is pretty much images and short videos (stories).

Again, I don't care which platforms you choose as long as you use one to get your voice out there. In addition to you, encourage others to go public with their views.

DRIVER #2: DEVELOP FOUNDERS

Ahhh, now we're in my zone. I love founders. They're the gas that makes the car run. They are the central element of this whole equation. And, we can never have enough of them. In fact, as I sit here thirteen years after beginning my startup community efforts in Raleigh-Durham, I continue to meet with founders every week.

You might ask, "But how many founders are there in my little city?" Researchers have offered estimates of anywhere from 5 percent to 14 percent of any given population. The wide variance is based on different definitions of an entrepreneur. Back to our definition for the purpose of this book—I am addressing high-growth entrepreneurs and not "Main Street businesses" like restaurants, dry cleaning shops, or retail shops (we'll cover these types of businesses in a separate book). There are others who are better at serving them and their entrepreneurial needs.

I think a smaller percentage is more realistic. Community builders should rally around the idea that 0.5 percent to 1 percent of the people in their regions are likely high-growth entrepreneurs. This potential population can be broken down like so:

- Active and Known Entrepreneurs
- Inactive and Known (Wannabe Entrepreneurs)
- Active and Unknown Entrepreneurs (Still operating in their basements and not part of your community)

- Inactive and Unknown (Don't-Know-It-Yet Future Entrepreneurs)

Think of the third and fourth bullets in this list as the part of the iceberg that's below water or what you can't see as described in the following diagram.

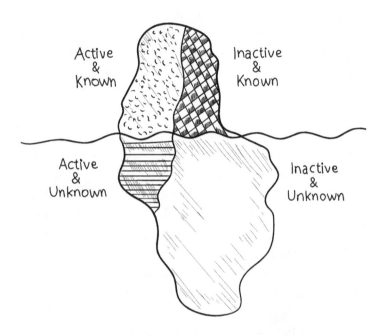

Your first task is to find the active and unknown entrepreneurs and bring them into the community, as they are operational and in need of your help, network, and experiences. They also instantly add their experience to your community as mentors. Some of them think there's no reason to leave their basement. Some of them aren't aware that there are others like them. Some have chosen to not engage, mostly because engagement activities aren't created in their best interest (rather, in the interest of the ESOs). It's imperative that you create activities with and for entrepreneurs and not for organizational vanity purposes.

I view this founder development driver as a means by which to increase the sheer quantity of local founders. Period. We can worry about quality and mentorship and investment capital later. I also think like a marketer, so maybe this classic marketing model can help you visualize what I'm after.

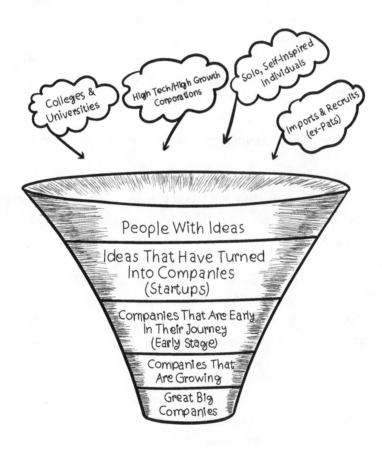

My thinking goes like this:

- Nobody can reliably pick the winners at the idea stage. If we could, wouldn't we all have invested in Google, Uber, and Amazon when shares cost pennies?
- Which means you cannot optimize or build a repeatable process for weeding out the bad founders or bad ideas.
- So, you might as well put as many ideas/founders in the top of the funnel as possible, as the more you have, the better the chance is that someone breaks out.
- I would also add that there's a positive flywheel effect when the numbers increase and the connectivity kicks in. By flywheel I mean that point where you don't have to work to build momentum—it just feeds on itself.

It's simply the law of numbers. More bets equals more potential winners.

One important thought that I want to share is around diversity and inclusion. If you agree that nobody can consistently pick winners, it further means that you don't know what the winners will look or act like, what their skin color will be, what level of education they'll have, or what age or gender they'll be. The wider you cast your net, the better your success is likely to be. Narrowing your choice to people of a certain gender, age, race, or background will hurt your chances to create a vibrant startup community.

When thinking about the types of activities that will encourage individuals to take their ideas and run with them, make sure you're providing a welcoming environment for a diverse set of founders.

As a leader of a founder-centric community, it is incumbent upon you to build multiple doors and windows into the entrepreneurial room.

Every activity I will share with you has an inherent natural target bias. Thus you must find ways to create a diversity of activities that address other constituents in your community.

IDEA PROGRAMS AND SEMINARS

As I speak from the stage, I always ask the audience these two questions:

1. Raise your hand if you've ever had an idea for a new product or business. About 98 percent do so.
2. Now, keep your hand up if you've ever actually started working on that idea or business. All the hands drop.

Why is that? In my book *Build the Fort: Why 5 Simple Lessons You Learned as a 10-Year-Old Can Set You Up for Startup Success*, I summarize this discrepancy with one thought: fear of the unknown. Basically, how can I start something if I don't know what I'm doing?

I regularly run my Idea2Launch workshops and have done so around the country over the past five years. The goal is simple: provide an understanding of how to take an idea and get it out into the world to see if it's any good. Along the way, you gain some confidence and a peer community group for those first few scary steps. These seminars are especially effective in nascent communities.

The key to success is a straightforward methodology (The Lean Canvas from Ash Maurya's book *Running Lean* is my template) shared by anyone with startup credibility.[17]

There are global, national, regional, and local versions of these methodologies to take advantage of and quickly put into place in your community. Just look around and ask peer community builders what they do.

OPEN OFFICE HOURS

Yes, I list this again, but this time it's for founders. Every city has a group of former founders. And every city has a group of wannabe or don't-know-it-yet future founders. Match them up.

I have an open calendar for an hour a week for video calls. (This was inspired by Brad Feld's random days where he would meet with founders for fifteen minutes. FYI, David Cohen pitched an idea called Techstars during one of these random days in 2005.) During these twenty-minute sessions we can talk about anything you want. Come prepared so we can maximize our time. When entrepreneurial leaders give back to the community in this way, we open up the top of the funnel for future founders to gather information about how to start something, the rules and the norms of the community, and more importantly, that there is a peer group waiting to help them.

These open office hours should be open to everyone. You should encourage everyone to take advantage of them and reduce any friction there may be around accessibility to your calendar. I

---

17 Ash Maurya, *Running Lean: Iterate from Plan A to a Plan That Works* (Sebastopol, CA: O'Reilly, 2011).

use two tools to set this up. The first is a calendar link from my website that lets you arrange our meeting. The second is an automated email reply that includes the same link.

STARTUP WEEKEND

Led by local enthusiasts but supported by Techstars, a Startup Weekend is a fifty-four-hour event (Friday evening through Sunday afternoon) that gathers locals from the startup community to build a crude version of a business—in fifty-four hours. These weekends are fun, full of energy, and very welcoming. Said another way for the purposes of founder development, a Startup Weekend is an activity that enables new founders to try on the entrepreneurial suit without quitting their jobs. At this time, there are close to a thousand of these events around the world. Some of them are open to all ideas, and some are themed around an industry (health care) or gender (women only). All you need is three to four leaders to commit, and Techstars will help you with standing it up. I think every city of size should be running several of them a year.

PITCH COMPETITION

A staple of universities and colleges, the pitch competition is an easy way to elevate entrepreneurs into the local spotlight. Some provide prize money to winners (which isn't necessary, but it can be a way to encourage better companies). Like Startup Weekends, pitch competitions can be limited to a certain audience (college or industry). In Indianapolis I witnessed seventy-two companies deliver one-minute pitches.

One method I witnessed was to use judges, which can help bring in a better crowd, then have the audience vote. I've also seen reverse pitches, where people pitch the worst idea and pick a winner...or is it a loser?

As long as you don't get caught up in the idea that a pitch competition will actually be a critical milestone for the company or the community, you're safe. I see them as another way to gather the tribe and invite others to the party.

COFFEE MEETUPS

Another favorite activity is the early-morning coffee meetup. The goal is to provide a regular destination where the community can gather, but more importantly, an easy entry point for new founders to find the community. Hold these meetups before work hours, and don't have much of an agenda except to meet people and network a little. Oh, and there's the coffee, too. If you can find someone to subsidize the coffee, that helps (a great role for the government or an NGO like the chamber).

A few founders embraced the Coffee Meetup in Columbia, South Carolina, and branded it "TechBeans." A local developer graciously provided space for the weekly meetups. That simple event created more progress for the founder community in six months than the efforts of the bureaucratic institutions had over the previous six years.

BEER MEETUP

The cousin of the coffee meetup is the beer meetup. With the same agendaless agenda, find a free place to host. Invite one of those startup microbreweries to bring a couple of mini kegs so they can drive awareness for their beer as a de facto sponsor. Food is optional. Monthly makes sense to me. Here's the thing about beer meetups with no agenda: they set an informal tone that reinforces a community approach, as opposed to an event with white linen tablecloths, select invitees, and speeches.

HACKATHON

For many of you, the thought of a high-growth startup is a software tech company. A hackathon is a version of a Startup Weekend but with more of an emphasis on developing a software prototype than a product or business. One of the more common hackathon themes these days is on some interesting public data that, when packaged and presented (like in an app), provides an interesting interpretation of that data. Find a couple of VPs of engineering or CTO types in the area and get them to lead a weekend hackathon. Connecting a group of software engineers over a weekend usually results in a few startup ideas that get launched that weekend or soon thereafter.

Regardless of the specific activity you're creating, augmenting, or expanding, there's an opportunity to build energy around the greater mission. Community energy is akin to momentum. Momentum drives confidence. Confidence is contagious. We refer to this as a positive contagion. Density of activity helps build a positive contagion.

DRIVER #3: DEVELOP MENTORS

Good entrepreneurs receiving bad or wrong advice puts a serious crimp in the future of those startup ideas—and the community. The problem is that nascent and developing communities do mentorship poorly. All the time. Mostly because they view mentorship the wrong way.

Mentorship is both a concept and an activity. The concept has its roots in the idea of community. The activity is something that two or more people do together.

If you think about the idea of community and tribe, you should think about the camaraderie and connection that members have as they have similar interests. With that similar interest comes a willingness, or dare I say, a responsibility to support one another. Mentorship as a concept is the idea that sharing your thoughts, feedback, experiences, and advice is a natural occurrence in startup communities. The breakdown occurs when new members aren't aware of that implied community support contract.

So, your task and the task of all members of the community is to be available and to create situations where new and veteran members can frictionlessly support each other. It's not just the give, but also the ask. For some reason nascent and developing communities are full of founders who think it's weak to ask for help.

Mentorship is creating activities that support both formal and informal connections. There are no rules around these connections. They can be proactive and reactive. They can be ad hoc and as needed, or they can be organized, themed, or structured.

The mentorship challenge for developing communities and some emerging communities is that leaders tend to take an overly structured approach. A perfect example is a program that *assigns* a paid mentor to a company for a period of time. This does not work! I'll explain why.

First of all, the mentor–mentee relationship has to be two-way for it to be effective. Getting assigned to someone breaks the mentor covenant. Second, paying someone to mentor creates a connection that has a transactional quality and again breaks the spirit of the covenant that we are all equals and that a great mentor relationship is two-way. Last, in almost every situation I've seen where there are assigned mentors, the program team typically finds individuals who are successful, late in their careers, or sometimes are retired executives from local corporations. Most of these folks have never started a company, and if they have, it was so many years ago that all the rules are now either irrelevant or just plain wrong. They unfortunately make for poor mentors.

The result: bad or irrelevant advice provided by someone who is not respected by the new founder. This in turn results in bad decisions by the founder or a total disconnect from the program and the mentor. From a community-building point of view we've failed the founders. Then we wonder why they leave for another city.

ACCELERATOR

A more recent and better-known structured mentor activity is the accelerator. As outlined in the definitions section, an accelerator has a structured mentorship program with an investment element. Great founders inherently understand that the investment dollars are nice, but the mentorship is the whole enchilada.

There's a stark difference between a great accelerator and all the rest. The problem is, you've probably never been involved with a great one, so you don't know the difference and they all look the same. They are not the same. The bad news is that if you invest or support one, as I mentioned before, you won't know it's a dud for several years (a.k.a. once the money runs out). This then puts the community back that same number of years and sours the mood for future prospects.

My advice? Do your homework. Visit the best programs, talk to their founders, and talk to founders from weaker ones.[18] Ask them about the nature of mentorship. A great accelerator can help move the community forward.

WORKSHOPS

Coworking spaces and universities are two of the most common conveners of workshops that mentor founders. These can be as specific as the following:

- What you do with your idea
- How to raise investment dollars
- How to hire your first employee
- How to run Facebook ads
- Whether you should patent your idea or product

They can also be more generic:

- What it's like to be an entrepreneur
- How to financially prepare to launch your company

---

18   Techstars, Y Combinator, and 500 Startups are three of the best programs.

- Whether you should partner with a friend or family member as a co-founder

There are a hundred other categories for workshops. I'm a huge fan of them because they provide a ton of value for founders along their journeys. Most workshops should be short (one or two hours), they should be free or inexpensive, and it's best when they have a peer network attitude so that post-workshop attendees feel like they can reach out to the instructors and peers for continued help.

The nature of the workshop should address the general needs of the community at that moment. For example, if your community is still building the top of a funnel for new entrepreneurs, focus on workshops on how to raise money from investors, as opposed to a more mature market need like how you hire and organize a sales staff.

OPEN OFFICE HOURS

I've mentioned office hours twice before, but this time I'm taking a different spin on it. Every community has a set of at least five to eight entrepreneurs who are either active or have been around the block a few times. Some are retired and sitting on the sidelines and some are pretty busy with their current endeavors.

There's an opportunity to coordinate some mentor activity when you convince these experienced warriors to give a couple hours a week to the community. Build a little website and tie it to their calendars like I did. Create "mentor Tuesdays" to promote consistent meetups. You don't need to curate the mentees—just point them to the website and have them sign up for twenty-minute slots. Establish rules (e.g., you can only sign up once a month or every other month; if you no-show you get banned for two months; no pitching for investment; come prepared; etc.).

Prepared and respectful mentees make it easier for mentors to stay involved.

These sessions provide new entrepreneurs access to the community and create an energy that builds confidence. Plus, they supply easy access to good advice.

One of the aspects of mentorship I alluded to earlier is who and what make a great mentor. Too often we picture mentors as grizzled old veterans who were executives in a prior life. These vets *could* be valuable, but in many cases their experiences or expertise is severely dated. They look good on paper, but there's no connection between what a current-day startup and founder needs and what they bring to the table.

More valuable is the entrepreneur who's several years ahead of the mentee. These people still have the oozing scars of the journey. Their experiences are closely relevant to the issues at hand.

I am a co-founder of Mapquest. It sounds cool, and it was an incredible experience with a fantastic outcome. I'm often asked questions like, "I am struggling with xyz and wanted to know how you solved this at MapQuest."

Well, I was involved in MapQuest thirty years ago. There was no Google, there was no Facebook, there were no mobile phones, and there were no cloud services. In other words, almost nothing from that experience is relevant today.

When looking for potential mentors either as founders or as managers of a mentorship program, cast a wide net and optimize more for recent experiences than lofty titles, long-ago exits, or some other fancy wrinkle.

PEER DINNERS

One of my favorite activities is a monthly peer dinner. The idea here is that a group of founders all generally face the same type of challenges around the same time. Let's get them together and build some group chemistry, some transparency in terms of sharing challenges, and ultimately, some peer support. As a community builder, maybe I can find a way to cover the dinner. If you're a government leader, this is a perfect example of an activity you can enable without trying to lead it. Because if you host it, you'll destroy any hope of its being successful: you aren't a peer entrepreneur.

Critical to the success of this entrepreneurial fellowship dinner is that it has to be a safe place to open up. What happens at dinner stays at dinner. No public sharing of what others have brought to the conversation.

THE NON-LOCAL NETWORK CONNECTION

This sounds like my new band name, but it means expanding your individual network by activating one outside of your city. What's amazing about every ecosystem is that each person has connections somewhere else. They can be friends, family, former workmates, customers, investors. Something we've been working on at Techstars is finding expats (people who now live elsewhere but are motivated to help those in their former cities).

There are many ways to activate this network to support mentorship in the activities we just addressed. Here are a few ideas:

- If you're connecting people every day within the community, now introduce those same insiders to someone outside the city. Yeah, it's that simple, but we never think to do it.
- Encourage other local leaders to do the same. One of the hallmarks of a developing community is that the critical mass of mentors is not available at this stage. So expand the network of mentors regionally or nationally and make sure a core group is doing this daily.
- Source LinkedIn or college or university alumni offices to make a list of expats. Proactively reach out and ask them if they'd be willing to serve as mentors. Create physical and virtual group meetings and share the wins, progress, and challenges for your community. Invite them to speak at local events and create an ad hoc event if they're in town for some other reason.

WHAT MAKES A GOOD MENTOR?

A few years ago, David Cohen, Brad Feld, and Jon Bradford captured a list of principles of what makes a great mentor. Later, Brad and Jay Batson expanded on these in a series of blog posts. These principles are baked into the Techstars accelerator model, and I share them with community builders all the time. They're called the Mentor Manifesto.

I am sharing these in the book not for you to use as a template per se, but as a reminder that you as a community builder are responsible for setting the attitudes, norms, and behaviors of the ecosystem. Mentorship is a critical aspect and you can help your community.

1. **"Be socratic."** The goal is not to end up with the definitive answer to the questions. Rather, you are trying to use the questions to set up a new set of hypotheses to test. You are at the beginning of a long arc of inquisition—use being Socratic as a continuous process to try to find answers.

2. **"Expect nothing in return (you'll be delighted with what you do get back)."** In give before you get, you enter into a relationship without defining anything transactional—you "give" in whatever form is appropriate, but you have no idea what you are going to "get" back. Now, this isn't altruism—you will get something back—you just don't know when, from whom, in what currency, or in what magnitude. You enter into the relationship non-transactionally and are willing to continue giving without a defined transactional return.

3. **"Be authentic/practice what you preach."** Focus on the phrase "practice what you preach." That's the core of authenticity in a mentor-mentee relationship. You are preaching regularly as a mentor. Do your actions match your words?

4. **"Be direct."** Tell the truth, however hard.

5. **"Listen too."** There's an old Irish proverb: "God gave us two ears and one mouth, so we ought to listen twice as much as we speak." That is useful to consider in the context of being a mentor.

6. **"The best mentor relationships eventually become two-way."** When I reflect on my best mentors, they are very long-term relationships where I hope they've now gotten as much from me as I've gotten from them. I call this "peer mentoring" and—while it can start as an equal relationship—it's magical when it evolves from a mentor-mentee relationship.

7. **"Be responsive."** Being responsive means more than just responding to email and phone calls. It means more than

being on time to meetings, closing the loop on things you commit to doing, and being intellectually and emotionally available to your mentee. These things are "hygiene issues"—if you can't at least do this, you aren't going to be an effective mentor.

8. **"Adopt at least one company every single year. Experience counts."** But nothing helps a mentor improve more than practice—continuing to try new things, seeing how they work, getting the feedback loop of mentoring a company, seeing the result, and helping some more. And most importantly, listening to the feedback from the entrepreneurs on what they think is helping them and what is getting in their way, slowing them down, confusing them, or undermining them.

9. **"Clearly separate opinion from fact."** Now, opinions are extremely important. But they are different from facts. This is especially important for a first-time entrepreneur to realize. It's equally important for a mentor to realize. When you are expressing an opinion, it's useful to frame it as such. When you are stating a fact, make sure your mentee knows it's a fact.

10. **"Hold information in confidence."** It's hard to know what is confidential, a secret, something someone is merely pondering, a brilliant new idea, something that conflicts with something else you know about, or, well, something that is going to make someone upset if it gets around. If you are uncertain, ask the person whom you got the information from.

11. **"Clearly commit to mentor or do not. Either is fine."** A fundamental part of this is a commitment to engage. Really engage. As in, spend time with the founders and the companies. It doesn't have to be all of them—but it has to be deep, real, and with a regular cadence.

12. "Know what you don't know. Say I don't know when you don't know. 'I don't know' is preferable to bravado." When asked about something structural, even though I've had lots of different experiences, read a zillion magazine articles over the years, and might have some opinions, as a mentor I'm quick to say, "I don't know," unless I'm confident that I do. When I find myself in an "I don't know" situation as a mentor, I immediately start trying to figure out who I can refer the entrepreneur to who might know something about the situation. And, just because I don't know doesn't mean I'm not curious about finding out more. I'll often stay engaged and hear what the mentor has to say, just so I get the benefit of having more data in my head to play around with in the future.

13. "Guide, don't control. Teams must make their own decisions. Guide but never tell them what to do. Understand that it's their company, not yours." A lot of mentors are successful CEOs. As CEOs, they are used to being in control. However, in the context of being a mentor, they don't control anything. The best they can do is be a guide. In the context of being a mentor, you still get to make one decision, but it's a different one. You get to decide whether or not you want to keep being a mentor. Assuming you do, your job is to support the founders, no matter what.

14. "Accept and communicate with other mentors that get involved." Move beyond whatever your past is and accept each other as a mentor in a new shared context.

15. "Be optimistic." As a mentor, your job is not to solve a founder's problem. It's to help. It's to listen. It's to provide feedback and data from your experience. You can do this from many different perspectives. However, given the stress on a founder, it's best to do this from an optimistic frame of reference.

16. "Provide specific actionable advice, don't be vague." At some point, the entrepreneur gets stuck but you want them to find their answer, which you support through stories from your experiences. This can be construed as vague in a crisis moment. Take a moment and try and deliver some advice that is more actionable without making their next decision for them.

17. "Be challenging/robust but never destructive." The moment you go beyond trying to get your point across to the entrepreneur and do something outside that moment that is less-than-supportive, you've stopped being a mentor. You are now simply a judge.

18. "Have empathy. Remember that startups are hard." As a mentor, be aware when to suspend or defer your advice or judgment. The entrepreneur you are mentoring may not be in a head space to hear your solution. Mentoring is often an emotional rather than a functional or intellectual role. Take a breath and be empathetic, instead of jumping in to solve the problem.[19]

DRIVER #4: DEVELOP INVESTORS

The fourth pillar in our engagement model is activating investors. I must begin with the idea that this is one of the most discussed aspects of startup community building. The core of the issue is the effect that capital has on the success of any startup. A secondary consideration is that two key actors in the ecosystem (founders and investors) are hardwired to take a biased, 180-degree different view of the issue.

---

19   David Cohen, "The Mentor Manifesto," *Hi, I'm David G. Cohen* (blog), August 28, 2011, https://davidgcohen.com/2011/08/28/the-mentor-manifesto/.

I don't know one entrepreneur who doesn't crave easier access to capital. There is not one political organization leader who does not believe that more capital will help create more founders and that capital increases the likelihood of success for those same companies. The twin cousin of this thinking is that in order to create more capital, you can simply recruit outside resources to set up shop in your city. This tactic is a leftover from the economic development folks. I see it every day when smart and passionate local leaders market their communities, cities, and perceived winners as examples of how advanced their communities are. Investors, especially those from out of town, do not succumb to this tactic. Smart investors look for good deals. Good funds look for good deal flow (not sure what deal flow is?—check the definition section at the end of the book). Your community can't just set up a fund without having a support system for entrepreneurs.

The concept that more capital creates a greater chance of startup success is inaccurate; in fact, an excess of capital can have disastrous long-term implications for many nascent or developing communities. The adage "good money after bad money" is typically applied when investors hang on to an investment too long.

Let's twist that adage to "good money to wrong founders." There's a tendency for less-than-savvy investors (typically local or regional government or NGO leaders) to create a small fund to invest in local startups, thinking that all they need is a little capital to goose the success train. In every developing startup community there is a star founder or five. They look the part, they talk the part, and they are working their tails off to build their companies. They are the best entrepreneurs in the region.

The problem is that their ceiling probably *is* the region. Their understanding of the challenges that are ahead of them as they attempt to grow their companies is limited by the fact that nobody in the region has ever scaled a company to that level before. The lack of mentorship and next-stage capital will combine to most likely limit the company's long-term prospects. That initial investment will feel good for a while, but two or three years later the company will enter a zombie state (the walking dead). Now the good money is gone, and there's nothing to show for it. Worse, local institutions and high-net-worth families say to themselves, "Let's never do that again."

I'm not saying that capital isn't one of the critical elements for community success. Indeed, it's one of our seven drivers and thus worthy of intentional activity.

What every developing or emerging community requires is an active angel community. Local angels serve as the first real investors for a company (outside of friends and family). Professional investors will rarely be the first investors in a company, local or not. Angel investors typically get involved at what's called the seed round, and this label should tell you everything about investing.

The good news is that every town and city has a population of high-net-worth individuals who have the means to do seed investments. Your challenge is to unlock this group. Start by inviting them to your coffee meetups or any other networking activity.

ANGEL AWARENESS

The first task of any community leader is to build awareness among the local high-net-worth population. For many this is a daunting task—how do you get access to these people, who normally are pretty quiet, don't speak your language, or don't understand high-growth entrepreneurship?

Well, it's time to put your big-person pants on and head to the dance. The good news is that there's already precedent with these individuals and families for supporting community activity. The new performing arts center or the nonprofit support or the college endowment are all examples of engagement based on a person's love of their community. Your challenge is to simply make them aware of what a high-growth startup is, why it's important for their community, and the different ways they can engage and support the startup community.

But first we need to find them. Think like that ten-year-old looking for materials for the fort. No fear. It's just a task. Use your network. Make a list. Get introductions. Set up an informal meeting over coffee or lunch. Tell the story of what and why, and build the fort.

For most, this is new territory, so make it easy on them. Here are some low-friction ways to build awareness.

DEAL FLOW

The most significant element of current and future angel investor participation is access to quality deal flow. Get to know this concept, as it's the lifeblood of every active investor. Deal flow refers to the quality and quantity of investment opportunities, and more of both is always better.

I like to focus on the word *flow* in that phrase. As a community builder, you are tasked with optimizing the flow of many things. For investors, they want to see a steady flow of opportunities. What does this mean for you? It's easy: create or facilitate a better flow of investment opportunities to investors.

There are a number of ways you can play an active role here:

- Introduce entrepreneurs and investors. A warm introduction goes a long way toward speeding up connectivity.
- Build deeper relationships with investors to best understand their sweet spots. The better the connections, the more credibility you'll generate for future introductions.
- Invite investors to local meeting spots for group activities.

ANGEL DINNERS

Most people find that sharing food is a way to create an informal, non-status-oriented activity. So once you have a list going and you've had some one-on-ones to share what you're trying to accomplish, invite them to a small group dinner. My format would be one or two active angels plus four to six potential angels, and of course a host. Grab a back room at a restaurant or even host it at your house. Don't overthink it—it's just an informal gathering of like-minded friends. The agenda can be as simple as prompts from the host asking why current investors do this, how they do that, and what impact these things have on their lives and their community. It's not a sales pitch, it's just sharing stories. Interested new investors will engage if they feel it. One other option to spice things up is to invite a current entrepreneur to light-pitch their company.

ANGEL GROUP

Many times, angels want to make investments as a group, as opposed to individually. I highly recommend joining or creating an angel group for two reasons:

1. The first is to help new investors who haven't built up enough experience and feel more comfortable as a member of a more seasoned group. It's a great way for them to learn.
2. Another reason to create an angel group is so it can serve investors who don't have deep pockets. New angel investors think they can consistently cherry-pick winners. Absolutely not true. Nobody can consistently do this at the seed stage. The best angel investors make twenty to thirty investments over a multiyear time frame. So if you have less cash, pool your money with others and put yourself in a position to be an investor in thirty companies instead of three.

There are a couple different kinds of angel groups and, frankly, community builders shouldn't care too much which vehicle the locals choose.

There are two basic types of angel funds. One is a pledge fund. In this vehicle, members pay a nominal annual fee to be part of the club, and a smaller group steps up to organize monthly meetings and select a handful of entrepreneurs to pitch. After the pitch, the angel group leaders ask for a show of hands of who is interested in potentially investing in the company and how much they could be in for, and then they form a due diligence subgroup to bring the investment decision to a head. The key is that other than the nominal annual fee, investors can make individual decisions when allocating their dollars.

An angel fund is simply a dedicated fund made up of a group of angels. In this vehicle, investors have committed an amount of money to the fund. A similar executive group or committee screens companies and brings them to the entire group to form a due diligence subgroup, and in most cases the executive group makes the final decision. Collectively angel funds can market themselves as having a $1 or $2 million fund available to local companies.

Again, it really doesn't matter whether angels invest individually or as a group when thinking about the startup community. Thus, your role is simply to create awareness of why and how, then convene interested parties in whatever vehicles make sense.

OUTSIDE INVESTORS

As I mentioned previously, I am not a fan of recruiting professional investors to your city in hopes that they'll fulfill the capital needs of your community. To try this only shows an ignorance of the motivations and incentives of those investors.

The only exception to this are the managers of national seed accelerator programs. I am most familiar with Techstars, but this applies to any national program (as opposed to the one-off local versions of the accelerator). At time of writing, Techstars has fifty programs operating around the world. Which means there are a hundred investment-seeking managers (each has a managing director and a program manager) who are spending nine months of the year recruiting and selecting the best companies for their programs.

For this team, it's all about deal flow. They will typically see about a thousand applications and speak to hundreds of entrepreneurs every year. This is an opportunity for you as a community leader to help your local startups. Reach out to these accelerator managers and either introduce your local entrepreneurs to them or convince them to come to your town and set up a day of meetings with them.

In 2017, I invited Amos Schwartzfarb and Natty Zola, at the time both managing directors of Techstars accelerator programs in Austin, Texas, and Boulder, Colorado, respectively, to come to Raleigh-Durham for two days. Each was set up with twenty companies per day in short, get-to-know-them meetings. At night on day one, I pulled together a social where each got a chance to share their thoughts on entrepreneurship. I believe four companies got into their programs. They always asked to come back every year.

Like other activities, can you arrange, cajole, fund, organize, inspire, and activate others to step up? Without an active set of angels, founders will pick up and move to a community where the investment activity is greater and access is seamless.

Outside of the accelerator program, there are very few ways to recruit investors to your area. Why? It's pretty simple. It's the cross section of value versus time. At the nascent and developing stage of your community, you don't have enough good companies for them to see. Remember, they see hundreds of companies a month, many from their own offices, where founders travel to see them.

Investors are basically followers, which means they'll lag behind the startup company development progress in your city.

With this in mind, how can you begin to build some awareness for your local founders (and, in part, the startup community)? Start by showcasing your founders in unique ways.

- Pay for individual founders to travel to the investor's city.
- Create a showcase "roadshow" event of your best companies in mature investor cities (New York City, San Francisco, Los Angeles, Boston, Austin, etc.).

Note: You need to be realistic about the maturity of your companies and their founders. Find ways to level set them against what investors are thinking today. The worst thing you can do is showcase a level-three founder or company to an investor who regularly sees companies that are level seven to ten.

I've seen a few interesting attempts to recruit a group of investors to a developing community. I want to share that this takes an extreme amount of effort and has to hinge on something so obviously unique that the value is crystal clear.

A few ideas:

- Orient the event around a highly technical topic (Quantum Computing, Web3, Blockchain, etc.).
- Orient the event around a unique local asset (Golf, Nightlife, Gambling—think Pinehurst, Miami, and Las Vegas as examples).

DRIVER #5: ENGAGE CORPORATIONS

Local corporations are one of the largest assets in your community. If you think about it, your group of corporations is unique to your area—no other city has the same list. The challenge for community builders is to encourage a meaningful interaction between your startup community and corporate staff. I've seen this happen in many different ways with just as many incentives and motivations. Let's dive in.

WHY SHOULD LOCAL CORPORATIONS CARE?

Read this segment carefully and you can thank me later for unlocking the key to this ecosystem pillar. Today's corporations are nervous. Very nervous. Tech advancements are changing the way they do business. Quoting Marc Andreessen, "Every company is a tech company today." It seems like competitors are winning that race and that your local corporation feels woefully behind. The issue is further exacerbated by the truth that technical talent is missing from the region. (It turns out that there is not enough tech talent everywhere and that your city is no better or worse than others. Addressing that issue will be left for another day or maybe another book.)

In nascent communities, corporations might imagine community startup efforts as competition for employees or ideas. They would be wrong. A strong high-tech, high-growth ecosystem creates innovation energy that waterfalls to everyone in the region. Corporations will have access to hundreds of startups acting as free R&D departments, a larger pool of talent in technology and growth marketing, and an exciting community to engage their employees, spouses, and children.

When it comes to the adoption of new technology, corporations are handcuffed by a lack of innovation. They all feel like they're chasing rather than leading. Innovation is a big word that means many things to many different people, which doesn't make it any easier to build a culture that promotes it in corporations.

The biggest challenges confronting corporations today are talent recruitment and innovation.[20] Engagement with the startup community can play a large role in addressing both of these needs. That is your lead-in.

There are obvious and compelling activities a corporation can choose to deepen their engagement. The impact that cascades to all involved parties is immeasurable. Your task is to connect these disparate communities for the betterment of both, a classic need that simply needs a passionate broker.

My efforts in Raleigh-Durham (and countless other people of course) in less than fifteen years resulted in these announcements in 2021 and 2022:

1. Apple picks are for $1B expansion; three thousand new jobs; average salary to be $187,000.[21]
2. Google announces engineering expansion; one thousand new jobs.[22]
3. Facebook (Meta) planning significant presence in Durham.[23]

---

20 Charles Mitchell and Steve Odland, "Survey: CEOs Are Worried about 3 Things This Year—and No. 1 Is Whether You Plan to Quit," Make It, *CNBC*, January 28, 2019, https://www.cnbc.com/2019/01/28/the-3-biggest-challenges-facing-ceos-in-2019-and-how-to-solve-them.html.

21 Adam Owens and Rick Smith, "Apple Picks Triangle for $1 Billion Campus, Thousands of High-Paying New Jobs," WRAL News, April 26, 2021, https://www.wral.com/apple-picks-triangle-north-carolina-for-new-campus/19646410/.

22 Sarah Krueger, "Google Picks Durham for Engineering Hub, Aims to Create 1,000 Jobs," WRAL TechWire, March 18, 2021, https://wraltechwire.com/2021/03/18/google-picks-durham-for-engineering-hub-aims-to-create-1000-jobs/.

23 Julian Grace and Sarah Krueger, "Facebook's Parent Company Meta Planning 'Significant Presence' in Durham, Sources Say," WRAL TechWire, June 6, 2022, https://wraltechwire.com/2022/06/06/facebooks-parent-company-meta-planning-significant-presence-in-durham-sources-say/.

These are economic development leaders' dream wins. But they could not happen without the development of a startup community and entrepreneurial ecosystem.

THE CORPORATE MENTOR

Newly formed and launched startups crave mentorship, which we already covered. Almost every corporation has a multitalented staff with functional experience in a number of areas. Think social media marketing or financial modeling or software development. Don't think of strategy or fundraising or more abstract corporate constructs.

Corporate executives can impact your startup community. Look no further than their staff; find ways to encourage them to #givefirst of their time. What's a couple hours a week to a handful of companies? Think about what the corporate staff will get out of the relationship (e.g., a cutting-edge view of entrepreneurship, the energy of the startup life, visibility into products or services that could benefit their department or company).

There are many ways to create the connection:

- Reach out to your local entrepreneur organizations and offer office hours to their constituents.
- Find a couple of local serial or successful founders and use them to set up connections.
- Find some local investors and ask them where you can help; also ask them to make connections with their portfolio companies.
- Work with local entrepreneurs to create an event and introduce your staff's skills. Invite the startup community for

free beer and food to foster natural connections (don't over-engineer these connections).

ALPHA | BETA | FIRST CUSTOMER

As a long-time entrepreneur, I can share that my biggest fear in launching and growing a company is whether I can get my product into the hands of my target customer. In fact, I strongly believe that this is more indicative of an early-stage company's success than the product itself. Entrepreneurs who learn how to create "product-market fit" without running out of time or money win.

One of the most compelling ways to serve a local startup is by offering to be a customer of its product.

You as the corporation get:

- an early look at a potentially disruptive product or service that could improve your business,
- an opportunity to influence the product or service while it's in development,
- a relationship with the founders and staff that you can leverage for talent access, and
- an investment opportunity.

The local startup and founders get:

- a real customer with real needs who can provide feedback,
- a revenue stream, and
- access to executives and staff for mentorship, investment, and possibly recruitment.

SPONSORSHIP

I am the barter king. It is my go-to starting point for everything. But sometimes things cost real money. As a community builder, you will have to get financial support at times to stand up an activity. Look no further than the local corporation and its executives. Of course, it takes time. You just can't walk in the door, introduce yourself, and come out ten minutes later with a check.

Over the last few pages, I have outlined many benefits to the corporation for deepening the connection to the startup community. Hopefully by now you've built relationships with certain executives and shared with them what those benefits are. Remember, it takes time to build the intersection of trust and credibility in relationships.

When corporations sponsor events, they typically receive brand awareness via logo placement on websites, at-event materials, or swag. But don't stop there. Giving one of the executives a few minutes to speak about their company is a great way to entice them to support.

THE CORPORATION AS FUNDER

Some corporations and their executives are motivated to take a larger role in the community by making direct investments. There are typically two ways that they do this:

1. Directing dollars from the corporation to the company
2. Participating in a local venture fund

I haven't seen many examples of corporations investing directly so far. It takes a high level of experience to do it right, and not many executives have that. In addition to the lack of experience, corporate executives aren't built to take risks in areas in which they have little experience. This one-two punch makes this scenario fairly unlikely.

More and more often, local corporations are investing in local venture funds. Blue Cross/Blue Shield and Red Hat are examples in Raleigh-Durham; Cox Communications is an example in Atlanta, and there are countless others around the globe. When done correctly, local investing seems to check all of the boxes and alleviate the above-mentioned concerns. My first piece of advice is to invest in funds whose managers are experienced investors themselves. Look for managers with deep relationships in the community. Corporate executives should be given access (not control) to portfolio companies, due diligence, and general operations so they can learn as much as possible.

MERGERS AND ACQUISITIONS

Every corporation experiences a time when it needs a service, a product, or a team of people to either defend their position or grow the company. We call this a "make versus buy" moment. A corporate executive's prior involvement in the startup community should inform their decision. Whether it was the sponsorship of an event or their investment into a local fund that provided them with access to startups and their founders, these executives should now have a window from which to broaden their M&A interests.

Great decisions are made from great information, and great information comes from awareness, education, and access.

DRIVER #6: ENGAGE UNIVERSITIES

Almost every town has a college or university within its greater metropolitan region. The core mission of every one of these institutions is to prepare students for their careers. Today, more than any other time in my life, those students are looking to entrepreneurship. I've been working with colleges and universities in support of entrepreneurship for over a decade.[24] The interactions leave me both excited and frustrated with the future opportunities before us.

These higher-learning institutions have within their walls an eager group of students searching for knowledge, purpose, and direction. By definition this student-state is ripe for creating awareness of entrepreneurship.

But at the same time, these institutions are organized in silos and led by faculty who are incentivized to maintain those same silos. Graduates pursuing entrepreneurship don't help the college's traditional rankings (there's no placement or salary to point to when *U.S. News & World Report* comes calling). Entrepreneurship doesn't fit into any one box (or college or department). It's not an art thing—but it could be. It's not an engineering thing—but it could be. It's not a geography thing—but it could be. And it's absolutely not just a business thing, though of course it has elements of business. That's just the curriculum layer. What about commercializing research? What about alumni offices that are only incentivized to connect students to jobs on Wall Street as opposed to starting their own companies?

This is your challenge as a startup community builder.

---

24 University of North Carolina, Chapel Hill; Duke University; NC State University; West Chester University; University of South Carolina; Benedict College.

As I see it, there are a handful of knowledge systems within colleges and universities that are able to drive local innovation and potentially result in playing a key role in entrepreneurship:

1. Educating and training students (computer science, marketing, engineering)
2. Developing potential products from science, research, and experimentation
3. Encouraging and even facilitating a problem-solving mindset across department and class boundaries
4. Actual company formation

Finding ways to connect students, staff, and faculty to the community is task one. Finding opportunities to support researchers, inventors, and staff at the intersection of their interests and entrepreneurs is task two. Rant over. :-)

Somewhere deep in the bowels of every college or university is someone who is carrying the flag of entrepreneurship. It may be a small flag, but it is a flag. We need to find them. We need to connect with them. We need to support them. We need to elevate them within those walls.

HOW TO TEACH ENTREPRENEURSHIP

Entrepreneurship cannot be taught in the classroom from a book. Period. It's an immersive experience. Let's be honest though, these institutions must follow a certain protocol that includes a curriculum, testing, and grading. So how can you help reconcile these challenges?

For those community builders creating better engagement with colleges and universities, it is your responsibility to share today's best practices for teaching entrepreneurship. The good news is that this is your door into their world. The best leaders want more help connecting with the interests of today's students. The most compelling classes I've been involved in get the students out of the classroom and into the business world to see and hear from actual entrepreneurs. Grading is based on interviews conducted, insights gained, and usage of the Lean Canvas oriented around their individual or group business idea.[25]

GUEST SPEAKING

More and more today, universities are supported by instructors from the private sector as opposed to tenured professors. This is very common for entrepreneurship classes.

One of the best ways to connect students and faculty to the startup community is for active or serial entrepreneurs to come in and share their experiences. This connection has both short- and long-term benefits:

- Students get real-life anecdotes to form their understanding.
- Students get real feedback on their ideas.
- Guest speakers facilitate connections to local events in person.
- Guest speakers find talent for their current activities.
- Instructors get to curate a wide variety of experiences, voices, and opportunities for their students.

---

25 https://leanstack.com/.

COMMUNITY, MEET STUDENTS

The biggest wall to break down is the one between the college or university and the rest of the world. This wall needs to be gone. You have to drive that forward.

The first task is to find ways to get interested students to the local events. Startup Weekends, Job Fairs, Hackathons, TEDx, and Tech conferences are all part of the bucket of activities I'm referring to. But beware! There are gatekeepers who want to prevent that for silly reasons. This is a raging example of the complicated mindset at play.

One way to get students to come to events is to go straight to them. There's probably an entrepreneurship club or a computer science club. Check them out and support their activities with sponsorship, guest speakers, or food and drink. Social media targeting is another angle in.

Another idea my business partner and I had years ago was to create an event just for college students. Our concept was to introduce them to former students of their alma mater who are entrepreneurs in an informal event.

It's a lot more fun to share the successful anecdotes, but community-building experiments can also fail. In the fall of 2012, my business partner, Dave Neal, and I were running our investment accelerator when we read Brad's *Startup Community* book, which gave Dave an idea.

At every college or university, there are single-digit percentages of students who are wired for entrepreneurship. In Raleigh-Durham, we have three large institutions: UNC Chapel Hill, NC

State University, and Duke University. Why don't we create an event for students to showcase the region's entrepreneurship and at the very least expose them to what's around here? We held our first Triangle.EDU event a few months later. About two hundred students showed up, though most were from NC State, where we hosted the event. We arranged for buses to cart students from Duke and UNC, but nobody showed up. The event that night was reasonably successful, but not enough people saw its value, so the event sizzled out.

CURRICULUM

I mentioned that creating, staffing, and teaching entrepreneurship is challenging for colleges and universities. Some are doing it very well and some are still getting up to speed.

Your job as one of the local community leaders is to create awareness and opportunity. There are a few ways to connect college and university actors to today's best practices:

- Blackstone LaunchPad program
- Former successful entrepreneur as instructor
- Best practices and learning from peer institutions

TECH TRANSFER/UNIVERSITY IP

"There is gold in them there hills" goes the old cliche. In just about every university there is gold to be mined. I jokingly share that in terms of commercializing university research, there's Stanford and MIT, and everyone else is tied for last. Relax, I'm not disparaging your university or the excellent programs it has in place today. It's just that there is so much more gold for universities to mine.

There's a fundamental gap that naturally exists for you that does not exist for MIT and Stanford. Silicon Valley and Boston have long-standing startup communities that have mature connectivity across the colleges and the rest of the ecosystem. Your city does not. No worries, Silicon Valley and Boston have just been at it longer. However, this is where you come in.

Though there's only so much you can do across the university as an outsider, there's actually a lot you can do to build bridges between faculty, researchers, and staff and the individual actors in your community.

I strongly believe that individuals are members of the network, not of the institution.

You crave not a connection with North Carolina State but with Haley Huie, who works at North Carolina State. You need to be connected to Christina Orsi, who led entrepreneurial programming at the University of Buffalo, not the amorphous thing called the University of Buffalo.

Frankly, it's much easier to connect to individuals, as they are likely to recognize that they may need something that you just might be able to help them with. Most researchers, professors, and administrators have fairly weak connections to experienced business executives, professional investors, and skilled actors outside their narrow interests. I am referring to marketers, product development folks, and salespeople as examples.

One simple task for you is to identify one-on-one and group activities that connect these actors. We can't predict where the serendipitous and meaningful connections will occur—we can only create the positive conditions for them to happen and happen in a positive and frictionless manner.

Though the task is simple, the execution will be difficult. Why? The actors involved here all speak different languages. They don't typically understand one another. The actors here think about the world very differently from the other actors, and they'll need a translator. That person is you.

PITCH EVENT

The longtime staple of the university/college entrepreneur play-book is the pitch event. If you got one rolling, don't stop it. It has value, just not in the way you'd expect.

Some view the pitch event as a springboard for getting founders and ideas off the ground and on the entrepreneurial journey, but I've rarely witnessed that. There are cracks between the intent and the delivery of a pitch event. This disconnect occurs among event organizers, the audience, and the companies. Many times I've been invited to judge, mentor, or just attend an event where the expectation of what I'd bring was not in sync with the university's or organizer's vision.

Students spend a semester developing a business plan, then they pitch it at an event as part of their grade. It isn't market friendly—it's academic. Hence the disconnect.

My observations:

- The idea pitch is a grading artifact for a class, not a real company ready to be launched.

- The founder has no intention of actually launching the company...unless I throw some stupid money at them.
- There are award grants of five thousand dollars to the winner, which is enough money to do pretty much nothing (and it certainly isn't an adequate incentive for launching a company).
- The university staff has no motivation or interest in seeing this idea actually launch (please stay in school and finish your education).
- The pitches are terrible, and little training (quality mentorship) has been given to the founders that matches the needs of the audience.
- The event is held at a time or place inconvenient to the targets (investors, judges, corporate innovators). As an event organizer, you should ask yourself, *Is this for me or for the entrepreneur?*

Get the event right and it can be a lift for the college, university, student entrepreneur, researcher, or staff. This isn't to say there's only one way to do it—just make sure that the expectations fit the format.

ALUMNI FUND

One of the more exciting university trends is the emergence of the alumni venture fund. The concept is pretty straightforward:

- The university supports a fund administrator (typically a former VC or associate from a VC) and possibly some part-time staff.
- Graduates from the university are solicited to participate and pay a nominal annual fee to be in the alumni investment club.

- Potential investments have a clear filter (e.g., one of the founders has to have some affiliation with the university: as a student, as staff, their parent is affiliated, etc.). I have seen this defined narrowly and broadly.
- The small fund team does the screening and recommendations to the alumni investment club, whose members then decide individually whether to participate.

Of course there are variations of this concept, but the boost in awareness, support, and general discussion around entrepreneurship has been invaluable.

In order for your startup community to grow beyond its initial developing stage, it must be able to leverage the local college or university. That leverage can come in many different ways, as we just discussed, but the task is tough as by definition, colleges and universities are walled entities with strong hierarchical structures. With every passing day new blood enters those institutions—people who have experiences and attitudes more in line with our complexity mindset. Find those agents of change, invite them to the existing activities, partner with them to stand up or modify existing activities, and create buy-in for a more cohesive startup community.

DRIVER #7: ENGAGE GOVERNMENT

One of the most discussed aspects of startup community development is the role government should play.[26] In *Startup Communities*, Brad pushes the government actors further out

---

26 There is little difference between city, county, regional, state, and federal government entities, and for the sake of this section, I am treating all of them the same. I also include private-public partnerships like a Chamber of Commerce, Economic Development, and other similar entities.

of the core activities since their election biorhythms don't fit or frankly support the longer-term vision needed to accomplish community/ecosystem goals. He has since expanded on this notion with a simple addendum: "Governments can and do play a critical role when their interactions are generally in a supportive role of the overall ecosystem rather than an attempt to lead the ecosystem."

The problem is further exacerbated in cities, states, or countries where the population tends to rely on the government for on-the-ground leadership. Though there can be some quick short-term impact, this government-led configuration unfortunately quickly runs out of steam. I have seen this firsthand where those early wins translate into "let's put more money or staff behind the purveyor of those successes." As time goes by, everyone begins to count on those entities for progress. The entity gradually begins to spend as much time running itself (fundraising, political lobbying, management oversight, etc.) as it does supporting its original mission. Staff changes further exacerbate this lost mission.

In order for your startup community to accelerate, the effort must be more citizen-based than government-based.

Why can't government staff be leaders? Brad has had to field this question many times since publication of his original book, and I realize I may risk the same fate here.

If you feel that my advising you to play a supportive role somehow diminishes your role, your influence, or your value, I ask that you consider an alternative point of view. To do that, you must dive deep into understanding the complexity mindset I've espoused so far in this book.

Need a metaphor? Let's think about parenting. At best we influence our children. Attempting to control or engineer our children's successful outcome is ludicrous and certainly not predictable. There are just as many failed attempts as there are successful outcomes. It turns out that we cannot make every decision for them. Every one of these small, seemingly inconsequential decisions collectively creates a path, and ultimately their success is based on this path made up of thousands upon thousands of decisions. Children are a perfect example of a complex system.

You are just one element of the overall ecosystem. You are not the parent, because there are many parents of an ecosystem. Remember not to get caught up in the fallacy that you or anyone else is the CEO or sole driver. Once you discard that notion, you can embrace your role as one important but individual contributor.

If I have you on board, then let's outline a number of ways that you or your department can put some wind behind the sails of the ecosystem.

CUSTOMER

Like corporations, the government has an opportunity to play a supportive role as a customer of the local startup's product or service. Just the sheer proximity of the startup to these entities provides a powerful opportunity to make change.

What often gets in the way is the machine of government, especially around procurement. Your job is to find ways to introduce, manage, translate, broker, facilitate, and troubleshoot these opportunities. Of these, the task that stands out for me is *translate*. There are probably no two more polarized operators than a government employee and an entrepreneur. They just don't speak the same language and don't operate on the same frequency. Someone has to translate between the two. To be an effective translator, one has to deeply understand both universes.

HOST EVENT

If there's one thing governments have, it's buildings. And buildings have lots of big rooms. Meetups, conferences, pitch competitions, and celebrations all require big rooms. Why burden community organizers with having to acquire professional event space when you have so many spaces already paid for by us local citizens?

Most of these buildings also have ample parking, which is a plus. Beware of restrictions like alcohol, or requirements like security, when evaluating various spaces.

SPONSORSHIP

Every organization has both budgeted and discretionary funds available to support activities. Even five hundred bucks goes a long way buying pizzas for the hackathon or Startup Weekend. Government staff members want to help—that's why many of them have this job. But you have to know whom to ask, and then you have to ask them. Not sure how to navigate this? Someone in town does—you just have to find them. Look no further than the organizers of events in town. Many of them are subsidized to some level by city/county organizations.

Think of sponsorship as akin to raising money for a startup. In order for these people to invest in you, they have to believe in you. For them to believe in you or your team, you must have credibility. Now comes the hard part. How do you create credibility when you're just starting out?

Identifying partners who already have credibility (organizational, individual, historical) is the best way to lift yourself. If the lift is too heavy, find some partners to work alongside you.

The good news is, the smaller the ask, the less credibility you need.

Remember, these organizations also want to be seen as supportive of their citizens and are motivated to find ways to drive economic prosperity. After all, it's their mission.

FUNDER

The difference between a sponsor and a funder is the number of zeros at the end of the check. As a government entity, funding is a much bigger deal and typically isn't part of some discretionary bucket. Creating the opportunity to fund something usually involves a lot of political maneuvering.

One of the most common startup community–funding vehicles is the venture fund. Done mostly at the state or federal level, this allocation of investment dollars can significantly change the landscape of the community...if done well.

Government staff should never make direct investments into startups.

There are two primary reasons:

1. They suck at it, which results in bad investments, and everyone loses.
2. The optics of investing in one company when you had to say no to many other companies makes for awkward situations.

You'll accomplish much more if you identify a set of experienced investors who can not only make better investment decisions, but can help founders and their teams navigate growth. It turns out money is only part of the equation, not the sole driver of success. Who knew? Complex thinkers did.

One of my favorite areas of government support is around skill development. Our economy is changing from being manufacturing-based to knowledge-based. Nothing new here. The problem is that second- and third-tier cities are the ones feeling the knowledge gap the most. (New York City, Boston, Chicago, and Seattle have already gone down this path. Buffalo, Raleigh-Durham, Des Moines, and Birmingham are still creating that path.)

I am acutely aware of the technology gap. At time of writing, there are over 178,000 new open technology positions across the United States according to CompTIA.[27] Every city in the country is struggling with how to fill these positions. Colleges

---

27 "Key Findings," CompTIA, accessed February 13, 2023, https://www.cyberstates.org/.

and universities aren't the answer, because the two-to-four-year format and relative costs are way out of whack.

For the past five or so years, a new education format has emerged specifically around software development. They are called code camps, code schools, or variations on that theme. They are typically three to six months, are fully immersive, cost between six and eighteen thousand dollars per student, and have a variety of subthemes. The good ones also have a strong placement service at the back end to help students roll into a job.

The financial lift needed to stand up one of these programs is pretty light compared to other training programs. There's plenty of room for government agencies to subsidize the cost.

Don't stop at software development though. Other areas of high interest these days are digital marketing, sales, and customer support. R&D is an interesting label that's bantered about a lot. There's a plethora of historical anecdotes, data, and case studies around the US government's directing R&D dollars that enabled the origins of Silicon Valley and Boston. It's a great story, but I don't think it's possible to copy that playbook today and get the same results.

It's another example of the "silver bullet" strategy that feels good to complicated system actors but that almost never pans out as intended.

It's quite common for large governments to think at a super-macro level—in fact, they should, so no judgment here. Super-macro thinking is best exemplified with my interpretation of a graphic from *The Startup Community Way*.

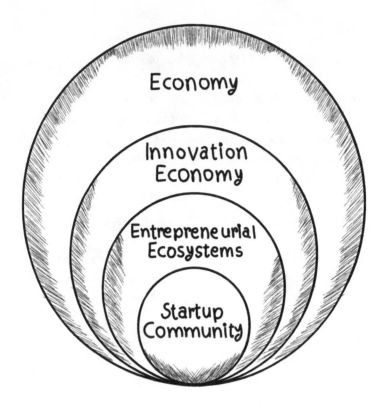

A macro tactic that addresses the Startup Community or the Entrepreneurial Ecosystem is to target the Innovation Ecosystem. Why not? If you figure that out, success will naturally come to the ecosystem, then community, right?

So, the first thing you do is build an innovation center on the outskirts of the city. The buildings are shiny with glass and cool atriums. There's a huge press event and all the players are there with their ties on. There's usually not an entrepreneur to be found. Then what? Three years later the parking lot is empty, and any semblance of a startup community has dissipated. You can't engineer a startup community or an entrepreneurial ecosystem or an innovation economy.

However, there are narrower fields of interest that when funded or subsidized by the government and wrapped around an existing research entity can have a positive impact. The key is to spend as much time connecting that program with entrepreneurs, business builders, and other actors.

POLICY

Full disclosure: as an entrepreneur, I am uncomfortable with this word. It is the epitome of top-down command-and-control thinking. But it turns out that many policies can reduce entrepreneurial friction, and a handful of policies can accidentally create it. As a budding community leader, you certainly want to see your government stack (city, county, state, federal) enact the good policies and remove the bad. Duh.

There are a handful of basic regulatory areas that should be addressed if your local drifts too far away from the standards.

Business Formation

In many areas outside of the US, entrepreneurs are viewed like Main Street business owners who are required to have a legal entity, business and operating licenses, etc., before they even start engaging with people. In *Build the Fort: Why 5 Simple Lessons You Learned as a 10-Year-Old Can Set You Up for Startup Success*, I outlined a methodology and a mindset around taking an idea to the point where you're ready to launch—i.e., the point where you should create your legal entity. Forcing entrepreneurs to create a legal entity and submit a myriad of business forms (and wait for approval) is a great example of a bad policy that creates undo friction for founders.

Entrepreneurs should be able to operate in idea validation mode for as long as they need without recrimination. Then when ready, entrepreneurs should be able to set up a new legal entity within a few days.

Business Termination

The other side of the business formation coin is business termination. Again, the gross majority of businesses will fail at some point. We need policies that support the termination of the company without undue friction or recrimination. Entrepreneurs shouldn't be targeted for any personal retribution. Some countries actually have policies stating that you can't close your business without registering it as an event, and the process takes months to finalize.

Both formation and termination friction have a significant impact on a person's decision to become an entrepreneur. Look no further than US policies that break down or remove regulatory barriers as guideposts.

In Peru, I witnessed an interesting culture/policy conundrum for founders. On the culture angle, older citizens had many bad memories of their federal government when it came to supporting (or hijacking) businesses. Younger citizens didn't share that experience, so they thought differently. Either way, there was a cultural phenomenon where both age groups adhered to the rules set by the feds.

Federal policy dictated that you officially get a business license before you started working on your business. This could take up to six months, which placed a significant barrier on startups.

They managed to reduce that to three weeks, which was progress, but unfortunately, another rule said you had to officially close a business before moving on (another unintended barrier to starting), an obstacle that could also take six months.

Tax Policy

In many regions of the world, including the United States, there are those who wonder if a more neutral tax code would incentivize more people to both become entrepreneurs and invest in them.

Research has shown that taxes and bureaucracy affect entrepreneurial development, as higher taxes appear to stymie firm development in emerging economies.[28]

Tax policy isn't just about incentives or risk mitigation. It can also be about understanding how entrepreneurs operate in the first formative years of their startup journeys.

One disheartening policy I've witnessed is taxing revenue versus profits. In a startup's formative years, there's almost always a reinvestment of operating profits (not taxable profits) into new features, new products, or employee hiring ahead of revenue. If the firm has to pay taxes on early revenue, those dollars can't be used to grow the company. Bad policy.

Many US states have adopted tax policies to incentivize angel

---

28 Benjamin B. Boozer and Taleah H. Collum, "The Effects of Tax Policies on Entrepreneurship in Emerging versus Mature Economies: Do Differences Exist Between Nascent and Established Firms?," *Journal for the Advancement of Developing Economies* 10, no. 1 (2021): 1–14, https:// digitalcommons.unl.edu/cgi/viewcontent.cgi?article=1045&context=jade.

investment into startups—one is by providing individuals a credit (25 percent to 100 percent) of the total investment. These incentives seem to come and go and also seem to be capped for both individuals and the total credits awarded per year. Why cap the total state credits, I ask?

This is clearly an area where government leaders can make changes to reduce monetary friction for both founders and investors.

Policymakers should consider the impact of the tax code on the entrepreneurial community as a vehicle for accelerating startup activity.

A Policy Strategy

First, let me reiterate that there is no single policy or policy strategy that works for everyone. In fact, there is evidence to suggest that some policies can have an adverse effect on desired outcomes. So be wary of the "let's throw everything against the wall" strategy. Don't assume that there won't be any losses by broadly testing various tactics.

Maryann Feldman, an academic at Arizona State University, and Paige Clayton, an assistant professor of Economic Development at Georgia Institute of Technology, sketched out a policy strategy that I like a lot.[29] Their thesis is that you should define specific strategies for specific stages of your community's maturity. They break those strategies down into federal, state, and local tactics.

---

29 Paige Clayton and Maryann Feldman, "Policy and Ecosystem Evolution" (working paper, 2020), https://maryannfeldman.web.unc.edu/wp-content/uploads/sites/1774/2021/04/Clayton-Feldman-Policy-Ecosystem-Evolution.pdf.

ACTION

THE FINAL TOUCHES ON THE ECOSYSTEM BUILD

So far, I provided you with an overview framework that introduced you to the importance of attitudes and not just actors and activities. I also outlined a maturity framework that's essential for determining both the assets and the gaps in your current state. Last, I put forth an engagement framework. Each framework establishes a mindset for your approach. Now it's time to put this mindset into action.

CHAPTER 6

ECOSYSTEM GAME PLAN

So far, I've walked you systematically through some important concepts:

1. I introduced the Build the Fort Five Principles to create a more simplistic mindset.
2. I further applied this to the complex system notion and that there is no specific roadmap, playbook, or recipe for success.
3. I introduced three frameworks that you can use to get started:
   A. Asset Framework (to inventory your region)
   B. Ecosystem Maturity Framework (to level set where your region is today)
   c. Engagement Framework (to outline, prioritize, and engage the seven key drivers)

Now it's time to bring this all together for you and your peers so you can focus on your actions. I think the best label for what you're building now is *game plan*. Game plans are adaptable and are based on the available data (which of course changes over time) and the reactions of the players in real time.

STEP ONE: COMMUNITY AUDIT

An oft-used cliche goes, "You can't determine where you're going if you don't know where you are." This is even more so for startup communities and entrepreneurial ecosystems. Your first task is to understand where your community is today so as to determine what needs to be fixed, altered, or augmented—or maybe you need to blow it up and start over with the BTF principles!

An easy way to get started is to simply make an inventory of everything that's currently going on in your city. Events, coworking spaces, venture funds, formal and informal programming, blogs, social media influencers, startups, growth-stage companies, the list goes on and on. This serves two purposes: one is a simple inventory so you can decide what to augment or add, and the other is to create a level of credibility for yourself.

Knowledge is power, and knowing what's up around your community is a superpower. How is this a superpower, you ask? Well, for starters, you'll be able to answer questions that come your way, suggest to people to attend certain events, or talk to specific actors who influence the future arc of the community. You'll be able to make the connections that will enable your community to grow and thrive. This serves the community, but it also serves you in terms of credibility.

Remember: serve with this knowledge; don't control the knowledge or your subsequent actions.

I do want to caution you that the purpose of gaining this information is to move the community forward, not to make yourself a gatekeeper, a know-it-all, or a power broker.

When discussing the needs of startup communities around the world, I've observed some common traits that may be preventing communities just like yours from moving forward:

- Investment capital is always front and center, especially when speaking to entrepreneurs. Entrepreneurs are often singularly focused on money: where to get it, how much to get, what it's going to cost them, how much they're going to make. For founders it's not the elephant in the room—it's the whole room. For many entrepreneurs, that's the sole reason for building a community. Their belief is that this is the singular barrier to their success. More capital isn't the panacea for growing more great companies. (Hopefully they'll come around to the BTF principles: that by joining together in a selfless way to make the community stronger, they'll win bigger than by just focusing on capital for themselves.)
- Developing new founders as well as retaining skilled and experienced workers is a clear need everywhere, especially around high-tech/high-growth companies.
- Density and connectivity are softer issues but no less critical ecosystem needs as both play key roles in organizing and driving long-term entrepreneurial success. Brad wrote a great blog post about ecosystem density that inspired me as a community builder in Raleigh-Durham.[30] Neither he nor anyone else ever calculated a preferred ratio (the total number of entrepreneurs and employees of entrepreneurial companies divided by the total number of all employees in a geography). In Durham during our ramp-up stage (2010–2014), I calculated a ratio of 1:7 (3,000/21,000).

---

30 Brad Feld, "I'm in Cambridge, Not Boston," *Brad Feld* (blog), January 25, 2012, https://feld.com/archives/2012/01/im-in-cambridge-not-boston.html.

- An ecosystem's culture, and by culture I mean the umbrella overlaying the network, is a key differentiating factor of any startup community. Every high-growth entrepreneurial community has a unique attitudinal underpinning that fosters innovative activities with a minimal amount of friction. Entrepreneurial communities cluster entrepreneurs and their feeder peers, accept failure as an integral part of the learning process, teach and support entrepreneurial skill development, promote jobs for startups, and foster public-private communication. These characteristics portray a cultural umbrella that permeates every activity, actor, attitude, and feature of a startup ecosystem. Culture ultimately drives almost all behaviors and outcomes within a city or region, yet it is always pushed to the side or forgotten.

In my work as a consultant (both Techstars and solo), I've developed a simple spreadsheet that helps me determine the maturity of an ecosystem. It contains a number of somewhat arbitrary sets of quantifiable signals. I'm not saying it's perfect or even scientific, but it is based on my work across quite a number of ecosystems.

This assessment helps form my recommendations for a community when I go in to help move them forward.

STEP TWO: COMMUNITY OR ECOSYSTEM?

I outline in the appendix a number of definitions that I think are important for understanding my point of view as well as facilitating a better understanding of the why, what, and when.

My partners and I have gone round and round with how to

define *community* and *ecosystem*. In our view, a startup community is a subset of an entrepreneurial ecosystem.

The Startup Community graphic in Chapter 5 is a good visualization. I also refer to this concept as similar to Russian nesting dolls.

But if you're embarking on a community- or ecosystem-building journey, where should you start?

Should you create a foundation for your ecosystem from the get-go or maybe make the decision that you can layer in the ecosystem ingredients after you've established a solid community?

I have a very strong opinion that you need a robust, healthy startup *community* in place before you layer in the other ecosystem elements. This view is based on my experiences that the people in the ecosystem who aren't part of the community have important and divergent day jobs. The startup community is but one of many different priorities for them. Hence, the time they allocate to our efforts is at a premium. For them, allocating their time to an effort where the community is not ready, or immature, or dysfunctional, will turn them off and they will allocate their time elsewhere and more dangerously disengage for a long time. At the very least, they'll look at our efforts with skepticism, which translates to lost opportunity.

To keep things simple and understood by all the people in the region, let us focus initially on assessing, building, or strengthening the startup community before we race ahead and begin ecosystem building.

I liken this approach to the one climbers take when ascending Mount Everest. Everest is a little over 29,000 feet above sea level, and climbers have to adjust their bodies to the increasing altitude (and lack of oxygen) in stages. These are called base camps. Depending on how you view the climb, there are several of these stops, all at increasing altitudes:

- Base Camp I is at 18,300 feet/5,578 meters
- Base Camp II is at 20,000 feet/6,096 meters
- Base Camp III is at 21,300 feet/6,492 meters
- Base Camp IV is at 23,100 feet/7,041 meters
- Base Camp V is at 25,600 feet/7,803 meters
- Base Camp VI is at 27,200 feet/8,291 meters

Total time on Everest is six to nine weeks to acclimate your body to the altitude at each elevation (base camp). This cannot be rushed if you want to survive! As I often say, there are no express trains to the top of Everest!

The point of this story is that building a thriving entrepreneurial ecosystem is a lot like climbing Everest. The activities you do at Base Camp I are different from the activities you do at Base Camp VI. And yet you have to start with Base Camp I in order to get to Base Camp VI.

Do yourself and your fellow champions and leaders a favor, and take a methodical approach to your community and ecosystem. Don't think that you're smarter than your peer leaders in other communities. Don't think that you can find that express path to the top of Everest—it doesn't exist. Successful startup community building is difficult and takes years of effort among a diverse set of people, all of whom typically act with their own best interests in mind (they are human after all). There is no express train for your startup community, there is no one tactic that will propel you to community stardom, and there is no silver bullet to slay the one thing holding you back.

STEP THREE: APPLY THE THREE FRAMEWORKS TO YOUR ECOSYSTEM GAME PLAN

The four ecosystem labels and their respective pie charts summarize my thinking around the priorities (at each stage) in which you should focus your activities to create the most impact. Think of the following charts as a guideline, not a detailed playbook or recipe. Take from these a means to set your priorities and focus your overall ecosystem efforts.

In addition to the activities to prioritize are the risks inherent at each stage of community maturity.

A great example of a priority at the nascent or developing stage is Investor Development. Getting local investors excited and engaged to make investment decisions and then not having a healthy pipeline of solid founders with brilliant ideas receiving stellar mentorship will cause you to lose those investors pretty quickly.

A risk at the emerging stage is being overly focused on activities that serve scaling companies and in so doing, accidentally reducing the pipeline for idea stage founders.

Note: The stages of maturity build on one another. As not to have to duplicate the foundational aspects of each driver at every stage, I will simply augment the words and ideas of those drivers at the previous stage.

NASCENT STAGE

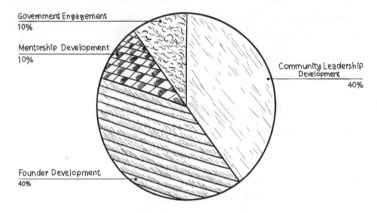

Government Engagement
10%

Mentorship Development
10%

Community Leadership
Development
40%

Founder Development
40%

Priorities

The two key drivers you should focus on at the nascent stage are Community Leadership and Founder Development; secondary are Mentorship Development and Government Engagement (which also means that you should de-prioritize Corporate, University, and Investor Development). Our thesis is that the right community leadership sets a foundation to manage the establishment and growth of the entire ecosystem. So set that first.

Equally important is the simple notion of creating more entrepreneurs. Founder development should build a long-lasting pipeline that serves all other actors in the ecosystem.

For many, this will seem unsexy and even a step backward. Fight that urge—these are investments for the future. A bigger pipeline of founders increases the chances of one of them breaking out and going big (which we all want, right?).

The last two drivers of activity are Mentor Development and Government Engagement.

As discussed, the best mentors are ones who have lived the journey. Find them, activate them, recruit them from your city and across the nation. Connect them with your founders and encourage more of that every day.

Government policy should be focused on building or supporting foundational structures (culture, connectivity, awareness, collaboration, and education).

Overall activities to focus on include dollars invested in events and programs that outline the Idea stage of entrepreneurship, and programs that simply connect current and future founders. You might also funnel dollars and time toward a developing support organization that aligns with the appropriate community goals at this stage.

A great way to summarize the cultural strategy at the nascent stage is to help build the foundation of the community. This may require standing up and *not* supporting dated policies; politically favored, long-standing projects; and leaders who don't exemplify the qualities outlined in this book.

Risks

The very nature of this stage—building the foundation for your community—many times yields the biggest risk, which is moving past the foundation building. If you don't build a solid foundation, the activities you add later may not have longtime support. Build a positive, non-zero-sum, #givefirst culture you can lean on when developing investors, mentors, and corporate partnerships.

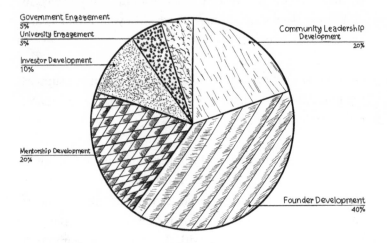

Government Engagement 5%
University Engagement 5%
Investor Development 10%
Community Leadership Development 20%
Mentorship Development 20%
Founder Development 40%

Priorities

By now, a number of leaders should be supportive of your mind-set (hopefully this one!). Figure out ways to divide and conquer. You will need help! Your ecosystem cannot grow with only your efforts. Nor should it. That is inherently limiting. This needs to be a community movement.

At this point the ecosystem leadership foundation is being built. Founders should be jumping in, a few supported by local angel investors, and company growth challenges (hiring, sales scaling, marketing, venture capital) dominate the local events.

By far, the single most important driver to focus on continues to be Founder Development. As a general rule, you can't have too many new founders. The tendency here for many leaders is to start to pick winners and put all your efforts into three or four breakout companies. Resist the temptation! You have no idea which ones are winners, remember? The market will take care of that for you.

Start to expand your Mentorship Development. As companies begin to grow, the nature of mentorship changes as well. Your mentorship programs need to address issues that confront these growing startups, but not at the expense of mentorship for *new* startups. Channel your inner improvisational comedian and operate under a "yes, and..." mentality. The existing programs AND new programs.

It's now time to build some activities around local investors. Chances are they're already holding events themselves. Great! So figure out how to support, augment, or supersize their efforts. Make introductions. Invite them to pitch events. Ask them to bring a friend to an angel dinner. Continue to make introductions between angel investors, CEOs, and local and regional investors.

I have also introduced University Development as a new priority, though at a secondary scale. My observations are that your local colleges and universities appear to be a great resource for your ecosystem, but this is a mirage. As a general rule, they're very difficult to collaborate with; they're hands down the most siloed institutions I've ever seen. They spend more time fighting one another than finding ways to integrate with the local ecosystem. But we still need to try.

At this developing stage, start by getting introductions to the professors and administrators who focus on entrepreneurship. Tell them what you're doing. Encourage them to read Brad's books (and this one too). Invite them to some of the activities outside the walls of their institutions. Ask them what you can do to support their activities, with no expectations. You'll need to bend a little to their thinking in order to get in and under their tent. Then influence from there.

Government policy should be focused on

- doubling down on programs to drive net new founders in the region,
- helping growth founders and their companies find new customers and markets (including the government at times),
- connecting founders and/or their CEOs to investors outside the immediate region, and
- building specific talent or workforce development programs that create or grow a skilled workforce for the local community.

The strategy at this stage of community maturity is to maintain or accelerate the activities that appear to be driving progress.

Risks

Great news. The founder pipeline is growing! But don't forget about upscaling mentorship. There are right ways and wrong ways to get and provide advice. The startup world changes quickly, and if your mentorship is only local, chances are that the advice you're providing is dated. Lean on regional or national mentorship connections to balance that potential void.

EMERGING STAGE

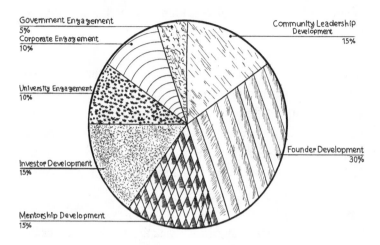

Government Engagement
5%

Corporate Engagement
10%

University Engagement
10%

Investor Development
15%

Mentorship Development
15%

Community Leadership Development
15%

Founder Development
30%

Priorities

The ecosystem is really kicking now. The Development work is generating a lot of new founders, and the energy in and around events is palpable. You can really see a sense of maturity among founders as they grow their companies. More and more of them are raising money (locally at first), and local and regional investors are stepping up to the plate.

All seven of our drivers are in action for this stage of ecosystem maturity, though they're at various priority levels of effort or prioritization.

The bigger and more critical emphasis should be in Investor Development. Your growing companies need capital. The locals provided the seed funding, but now the ecosystem needs professional capital. At this stage, one to three new micro (less than $50 million) venture capital funds are leading series A–type deals ($1 million to $3 million). Figure out ways to help them raise their funds. Introduce them to family offices, other venture firms, corporate CFOs, and local foundations. Raising a venture fund is the hardest thing I have ever done.

In addition, regional and national firms are starting to take notice. You can't recruit a venture firm to your area like you would a company. I've yet to see that happen, let alone work. But you can introduce your breakout companies to them. You can create unique and special events that they are interested in—and then introduce your local breakout companies to them.

University Engagement is also a growing priority at this stage. There are three general angles of attack that you should consider. The first is to build a tighter integration between entrepreneur classes and the community. Encourage your breakout company founders/CEOs to be guest speakers at the classes and events. This also means encouraging instructors to be on board.

The second angle of attack is to work with both the career development office and the instructors of entrepreneur classes to help build a pipeline of internships that lead to jobs at local startup companies. It wouldn't be for everyone, but there is a percentage of students who would love to stay after graduation.

The third angle of attack is what is commonly called Tech Transfer, or intellectual property (IP) Commercialization. Almost every college and university has a group that's doing some serious research. They're creating IP every day but generally have little to no ability (or motivation) to commercialize it. That's where the ecosystem can help. You need to build bridges between the business folks and the research folks. There are many ways to do that, from IP showcases to one-on-one meetings.

Corporate Engagement opportunities are ready to be harvested at this stage. This group is a critical propellant for moving from emerging to leading. However, they're also finicky, and rightfully so—they have businesses to run, shareholders to be accountable to, and employees to keep on task and on mission. So where does a startup community or entrepreneurial ecosystem come in?

My best advice is to start at the top and target executive leadership at local corporations. The best way to engage executive leadership is to show them elements of the community. As long-tenured businesspeople, they will not "get" startups and their needs, so it's your job to show them. Invite them to some events. Ask them to speak on a panel or judge a competition. Appeal to the fun part of their personality. Maybe invite them to a dinner with a few founders of various company sizes or stages.

As outlined earlier, there are many roles that corporations and their employees can play in the ecosystem. The actual role and the level of engagement will obviously vary from corporation to corporation. The bottom line is that you'll need their buy-in to build your ecosystem beyond the emerging stage.

My argument, especially as related to high-tech-growth companies, is this: A robust and growing tech ecosystem will provide a foundation that your corporation will benefit from as it evolves and requires more and more tech capabilities. Simply said, a robust tech ecosystem will be where you recruit your next tech employees from.

At this stage, overall local and state government policy should fade to the background or frankly get the heck out of the way.

The community has matured to the point where it's generally self-sustaining.

The whole self-organization state of affairs is an engine that feeds itself the fuel needed to continue its journey. I would suggest that this is a great time to reassess the ecosystem for weaknesses or gaps that could stall the work and progress made to date.

Policy tactics include the following:

- Drive cross-collaboration among the ESOs (look for unhealthy power structures or individuals, and use your influence to bring them back into the fold).
- Facilitate meetings among disparate actors who wouldn't normally convene (e.g., investors, corporations, and universities), including outside the immediate region.
- Identify large startup costs (natural business friction points) and lead private-public partnerships to reduce them.
- Invest in alternative education programs related to business scaling (marketing, sales, product development, engineering).
- Support new investment vehicles that are matched to the founders' needs and stages of ecosystem maturity (we don't need a $250 million fund in year two of our emerging status).

Risks

There is something pretty important with regard to leadership that I want you to be aware of at this stage of your ecosystem's maturity. There's a very good chance that the original ecosystem builders are starting to fade out. I've lived it myself both as a builder and as a consultant observing an ecosystem. In fact, one of the indicators of an ecosystem plateau is the awkward activity leadership transitions as leaders begin to disengage. Life happens. The mostly volunteer tasks of community and ecosystem building start to get in the way of our day jobs, especially when the day jobs change.

So be prepared and be proactive in building succession in events, programs, funds, etc. What do I mean by proactive? You have to start recruiting the next generation into these ecosystem-building activities before you need them to take over. We made this mistake in Raleigh-Durham about five years back, and, after suffering from a three-plus-year plateau, we're now fixing it.

What you can't do is assign someone to the leadership task. If you do, you'll be right back where you started, with the wrong people leading the charge. It may feel better in the short term, but making this mistake results in lousy outcomes in the long term. Be intentional with your efforts!

Another item to be aware of is the accidental personality change of your local ESO. By now, this organization has been a real driver for progress. But time is not your friend. Leadership will invariably change, and with that change comes a tendency to:

- hire someone who has a manager mindset,
- hire the longest-standing operations person in the ESO,
- hire someone who can help raise next-level funds to grow the organization, or
- hire someone temporarily from the board of directors who's a safe operator.

When we do any of the above, the organization begins to forget its mission: to serve entrepreneurs. The organization starts to believe that it is more important than the founders themselves. I OBSERVE THIS EVERY DAY! You must guard against that natural human tendency.

LEADING STAGE

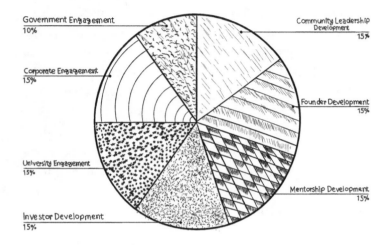

Priorities

If it ain't broke, don't fix it. Or something like that. In general, I don't think any of you need to worry about a decline in your startup community (like Detroit with automobiles, or Pittsburgh with steel).

However, I have seen community plateaus that last for months to a couple of years, and they need to be addressed; just be aware that it can and will happen to your community. It just makes sense that a complex system and many different actors who have changing motivations will conspire together to drive unintended outcomes—both good and bad.

At this stage, our seven drivers are all in play, though there may be some primary areas of focus (Founder, Mentor, Investor, University, Corporate, and Leadership Development/Engagement) and then trailing focus (Government Engagement).

Again, things are working. Right? Activities have a lifespan to them just like restaurants. They're hot for a while and then they get stale. To remain a leading ecosystem you have to recognize that what worked two or five years ago may not work now. And what works in another community may not work in yours.

What I would want for you all when you reach this level is a constant evaluation of what is working across all seven drivers with an eye toward making incremental improvements when necessary.

Our customers (founders) change. Old investors fade out and new ones emerge. Universities and colleges find new ways to teach entrepreneurship. IP and technology changes (e.g., Web3, crypto, blockchain, quantum computing) create new opportunities that need to be addressed. Community leader transitions impact and put stress on the ecosystem. And of course there are new politicians with new agendas every two to six years.

Risks

Everything is a small risk at a small level as a leading ecosystem. Each driver and its inherent activities invariably get stale. It's the natural life cycle of events and activities. So plan for obsolescence. Plan for succession. Proactively create space for new leaders to emerge.

CHAPTER 7

WE GOTTA MEASURE, DON'T WE?

I would be remiss if I didn't address the enormous elephant in the room. In multiple instances in this book, I've debunked common startup community fallacies. Measurement is the big enchilada. One of the biggest ever in my career, and I've tackled many.

I find that measuring the startup community is the single biggest myth, and many times the single biggest inhibitor to startup community progress. I think Feld and Hathaway in *The Startup Community Way* said it best:

> Startup communities must avoid the trap of letting demand for measurement drive flawed strategies. The most tangible and therefore easiest factors to measure in a startup community also have the least amount of impact on its performance over the long term.[31]

---

31 Brad Feld and Ian Hathaway, *The Startup Community Way: Evolving an Entrepreneurial Ecosystem* (Hoboken: Wiley, 2020), 183.

WHY WE MEASURE

Let's take a step back and try to understand the motivations of the manager's mindset and how it intersects with our motivation to grow our startup community.

What we really want is to reverse engineer those specific activities that are correlated with the local startup company's success so we can repeat those activities at scale. This is the engineer's approach to startup community building. It makes a lot of sense on the surface. Find those elements to measure, correlate them with successful companies, take credit for creating the activities that are aligned with those measures so we can secure more funding, rinse and repeat.

Today's modern manager mindset, which permeates government, corporations, and even colleges and universities, is based on the thought that what gets measured gets managed.

At its core, the idea from Peter Drucker in 1954 was this: Drucker believed that business leaders needed to embrace the "spirit of performance," among many other elements, by focusing on results. Along this path, I believe we have taught current and emerging business leaders that measuring results is a safe way to advance one's career, achieve success, and, most importantly, manage outcomes that are in your (individual, company, community) best interest.

Underlying this measurement mindset is the idea of control. Control feels good. It supports our ego and enables us to look like leaders. Leaders control their businesses. Great leaders control better than good or poor leaders.

This control mindset only deepens over time, and why shouldn't it? Those who continue to advance their careers are rewarded by embracing and mastering the art of measurement and its counterpart, control.

By the way, the only institutions where you continue to advance your career by measuring activities are the government, large corporations, and universities. This idea does not exist in solo and small businesses (which make up 99 percent of all businesses and 47 percent of employment today).[32] In other words, over half of our working population is not concerned about building their career.

So it is no surprise that when late-in-career institutional managers are either assigned or gravitate to the task of growing their startup communities, they bring a manager, measurement, control approach.

As consistent in this book and *The Startup Community Way*, we refer to this phenomenon as part of a complicated mindset instead of the complex mindset needed for startup community success.

THE TYPICAL USELESS MEASUREMENT DATA

So we measure because we have to. We measure because the funders make us as part of the package for receiving said funding. We measure because that's what everyone else does.

---

32 U.S. Small Business Administration, Office of Advocacy, "Frequently Asked Questions about Small Businesses," September 2019, https://cdn.advocacy.sba.gov/wp-content/uploads/2019/09/23172241/Frequently-Asked-Questions-Small-Business-20191.pdf.

There are two metrics everyone uses today: capital and jobs.

CAPITAL

The easiest, most utilized, and still imperfect data to collect for our startup community is the amount of capital deployed (investments) in our startup companies. Why? There are legal reasons. There are public relations reasons. There are analytics reasons (third-party organizations that make money gathering data so we can measure things).

The problem here is that the amount of capital deployed in a given time period across your startup community has absolutely no link or correlation to why the founder started the company in the first place. It doesn't address what activities, programs, or mentorship played a starring role in helping that founder take their idea from launch to scaling success or how they were able to secure those funds (e.g., actual company growth, fantastic pitch, VC introductions).

A great example of using capital to market yourself is this unnamed state agency. On their website they highlight the $1.003 billion economic impact they had on the state's economy from $4.6 million in investments. First, why the three digits to the right of the decimal point? Is it to show the supposed precision of their analysis? Second, this example shows how misleading metrics can be. I know of no investor who would turn down a $1 billion return on a $5 million investment. However, the actual investment data I analyzed shows that this state is woefully behind its peer states in almost every innovation or entrepreneurship category. Their $4.6 million investment has not spawned new entrepreneurship, the investment has not inspired out-of-state investors to invest in their state, and most importantly the stated impact of this investment is questionable. They are lying to themselves and the constituents that they serve with regard to their efforts.

Vanity metrics created by economic developers or entrepreneur service organizations have little impact on inspiring, developing, and growing entrepreneurs.

At best, capital deployed in a company (and a region) is a lagging indicator of an entire ecosystem's set of work. At worst, measuring capital deployed and using that as a means to determine the ecosystem inputs that drove that perceived success is pure insanity. There is no link between a region's deployed capital and its number of successful startups.

Research supports this theory—the amount of capital in a community has zero influence on starting new companies.[33]

Company success has many parents. So does company failure.

According to a recent CB Insights report analyzing over a hundred post-mortems:

- Sixty-two percent of the reasons for startup failure were not related to capital.
- Thirty-five percent were due to a lack of market need.
- Twenty-six percent were because of team dynamics.[34]

---

33   Paige Clayton, Maryann Feldman, and Benjamin Montmartin, "Financing Regional Industrial Emergence" (working paper, 2020). Check that statement against their research!

34   CB Insights, *The Top 12 Reasons Why Startups Fail*, 2021, https://www.cbinsights.com/research-12-reasons-why-startups-fail?utm_campaign=marketing_startup-failure_2021-07.

JOBS

The other most common measuring stick is the number of net new jobs that the startup companies have created. This metric is directly aligned with traditional economic development. Recruit in a mid- to large-sized manufacturing company and it creates a hundred to a thousand new jobs. Winner, winner chicken dinner.

The economic development goal with respect to creating local technology-based startup companies is clear. For every tech job, an additional 4.3 service jobs are created, versus 1.4 for manufacturing jobs. But as covered, this economic flywheel effect driver is again an output not an input.

Whenever we set a goal of "we need more technology jobs" and the subsequent monitoring and measuring of that metric, we begin to create a dialogue and an environment that skews our true goal.

What we want are excellent tech companies, which will typically create good jobs. Some of those tech companies will hire more tech people. But not all tech companies scale their employee bases commensurate with scaling their companies. And we should never encourage the mindset that more tech employees equals our innovation economy goal.

The best example to support this thesis is the story of Instagram. In April of 2012, Instagram was sold to Facebook for $1 billion in cash and stock. The deal netted cofounders Kevin Systrom and Mike Krieger hundreds of millions of dollars based on their ownership stake. Instagram had thirteen employees at the time of the sale.

From a traditional economic development perspective, Instagram was a complete failure. Those thirteen employees created about fifty-six jobs using our flywheel metric. "Yawn," says the local chamber of commerce president.

But what if Kevin and Mike lived in your city? They each have hundreds of millions to recycle into your ecosystem. They also have company scaling expertise and experience in selling out to one of the biggest companies in the world. So do the thirteen employees of theirs who went along for the ride. They too would create some trickle-down economic impact.

Give me an Instagram in my town every day versus some quasi-tech/service entity (an Apple data center with twenty low-paying service jobs) that can only scale with more people—but has a "we created jobs" story to tell.

What am I trying to say? Startups and startup communities are complex systems and, as such, there are many variables. Those variables interact differently in different places, and all of that merges to create startup success and failure. Measuring niche elements of the complex system that are easiest to gather and then developing strategies and tactics around those metrics is not a healthy approach.

MEASURE WHAT MATTERS

What I would like you to consider is building an approach that measures what matters. What matters most? If you've gotten this far, you should have a pretty good idea of some of those elements.

Assuming you're in the mindset I laid out over the past two-hundred-plus pages, you might want to measure the following things:

- Who is playing a role in the community?
- Who seems to carry the most influence?
- What activities are most attended?
- Which founders seem to be growing their companies?
- Where do people secure capital?
- Which vendors are having the most positive impact?
- Where do new founders engage?
- What community-positive attitudes are most pervasive?
- Which local corporation, government, or university actors are playing a role?
- Where are new founders coming from?
- Are founders leaving? Why?

Add another ten to fifteen questions around this mindset. And capital and jobs, as they have some value within the greater context of what we're trying to do.

The challenge you will find is that the things we want to measure, which are the things we think actually matter (inputs that increase the chances of meeting our goals), are very difficult to measure.

In fact, the only way I know how to do this well is to interview all of the actors on a continual basis. You know, talk to your customers! Bake that into your long-term strategy and you might actually measure the right things, and that data might just influence your strategy and tactics enough to accelerate your startup community.

THE NETWORK

I believe with every fiber in my startup community builder soul that the ultimate measure of a community's success is both the connectivity of the actors within the region *and* the level of meaningful relationships among the connected.

If you want a great gauge of where you are, where you're going, and which activities are ultimately driving progress, measure your network.

Rhett Morris and Lili Török, then at Endeavor Insight, developed the ultimate ecosystem network graph tools. These are best exemplified in a convincing piece of ecosystem research found in their report *Fostering Productive Entrepreneurship Communities*, published with funding from the Gates Foundation in October of 2018.[35]

The following graphic, constructed after they interviewed hundreds of actors in each city (Nairobi and Bangalore), reveals a compelling story. It illustrates the connectivity within the region as well as the type of connections and who the major influencers in their ecosystem are.

---

35 Rhett Morris and Lili Török, *Fostering Productive Entrepreneurship Communities: Key Lessons on Generating Jobs, Economic Growth, and Innovation* (Endeavor Insight, October 2018), https://endeavor.org/wp-content/uploads/2021/09/Fostering-Productive-Entrepreneurship-Communities.pdf.

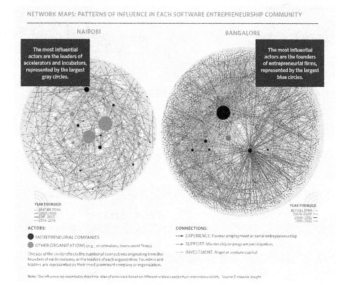

This research is expensive, time-consuming, and driven by experts. I use their services when engaging in a serious long-term engagement. But there are other ways to glean generally the same information without the rigor that Rhett and team brought to these projects.

In Columbia, South Carolina, I interviewed fifty to sixty actors (more than thirty-five founders) within an initial three-month period and another 150-plus over the rest of the year. My preliminary goal was to ferret out those same three questions (connectivity, meaningfulness, and influencers).

With an initial focus on founders, I was quickly able to map out a crude version of the above and determine the culture of the region.

Ian Hathaway and I are still working on ideas of how we can get this initial network map developed without a three-month, fifty-plus expert interview tour, but we have yet to put any of those into action.

FOUNDER SENTIMENT

Since we believe that successful outcomes for founders equates to successful outcomes for our communities, it makes sense to check in with founders to find out how they're feeling. Let me take a second to spin this around to the role of community builders. Wouldn't we want to understand whether founders feel supported by their communities?

Measuring founder sentiment is one way we can take a snapshot of how our founders are feeling about the activities, programs, and general support they receive. And since community builders are the ones creating those activities and programs, founder sentiment might be the best measuring stick for our efforts.

Founder sentiment can be measured as easily as by asking every founder a question like, "How are you feeling about the support you receive from your community?" I would provide each founder with a simple three-answer choice (in sync with the Net Promoter Score concept): great, neither great nor disappointed, and disappointed.

I would track each founder's answer over time, running the survey two to three times a year at the same time to remove any seasonal bias.

COMMUNITY BEHAVIORS

Ah, here lies the ultimate but elusive measurement driver for growing your startup community. Are the actors exhibiting the type of behaviors that create a better startup environment? Or not?

This book has outlined as many of those behaviors as I could identify, but I'm sure I missed many.

Tracking or measuring those behaviors is very difficult. They are personal. They are revealed mostly in one-on-one interactions, and they're open to interpretation because of their importance in that moment and the amount of influence that resulted from that behavior.

So, Chris, why did you include this?

I think there are a handful of individual behaviors that can serve as signals as to where your community is and where it is going. Here are two that I think are important and serve as signals for me:

- **The Brokered Introduction:** Great communities connect each other with little to no friction—I introduce people every day. In nascent, developing, and emerging communities, I believe in direct introductions. This method signals a level of trust among the three of us. Actors in leading communities may respond better to double-opt-in introductions.[36] Either way, there are ways to measure who's making introductions and how many they've made, and even their quality. I use

---

36 Fred Wilson, "The Double Opt-In Introduction," *AVC* (blog), November 3, 2009, https://avc. com/2009/11/the-double-optin-introduction/.

an app from one of the smartest former Techstars Managing Directors, Connor Murphy, called BRDG.APP. I encourage all of the local leaders I work with to use it as well, and then to share their activity within the community.

- **Influencer/Leader Attendance:** We take cues and mirror behaviors from those we respect. Running startup events and programming are the key activities we use to create value. When those acknowledged influencers or leaders show up, we see it, and a little voice inside our head says, "If they think this is important, then I think it's important." I cannot overestimate the value of just showing up. In nascent and developing communities that still have a patriarchal structure, many leaders don't feel the need to attend, say, a weekly coffee meetup. The signal that sends is painfully obvious. In terms of measurement, it's pretty easy to not only count overall attendance, but also the attendance of influencers and leaders.

CONCLUSION

Community leaders set the tone and approach that others will emulate. I want to end this book with a chapter that reminds us of the core thesis that Brad, Ian, many others, and I adhere to every day. It is the Boulder Thesis. These are our north stars from which everything else emanates:

1. Entrepreneurs must lead the startup community.
2. Leaders must have a long-term commitment.
3. The startup community must be inclusive of anyone who wants to play a role.
4. The startup community must have continual activities that engage the entire entrepreneur stack.

Let's augment these north stars with a simple game plan:

1. Inventory your region (activities, actors, and attitudes).
2. Assess where you are (four levels of maturity).
3. Outline a set of goals (based on ecosystem maturity).
4. Lead, augment, or partner on various activities that support one or more of the seven drivers.

5. Measure, review, and report progress to the ecosystem.
6. Reassess, reset goals, execute plans, and measure annually.

In this book, I have tried to provide a methodology by which you can play a leading role in your startup community. There are strategies, tactics, and lists. There are ideas, concepts, and game plans. Most importantly, there's a mindset.

Your task is to lock in on the mindset, share and support it with others, then layer in the activities that seem to be the most important to you, your peers, and the members of the community. Remember, there are no right answers, there is no exact playbook to follow, and there is no perfect outcome. There's only the process of discovery as you uncover what your community needs and rally the tribe to address those needs.

If you take only one thing from this book, if you need one north star to orient your actions, remember this: Founders First!

Good luck. I'm rooting for you from afar.

APPENDIX

DEFINITIONS (YES, IT'S THAT IMPORTANT)

Like many niche concepts, some words and phrases have different meanings for different people. You might find these terms to be fuzzy, unclear, or difficult to understand. You can come back to this section as often as you need.

CONCEPTS

Activities—all the organized endeavors undertaken to support entrepreneurs. Angel funds, boot camps, and coffee meetups are all examples.

Actors—members of the community and the ecosystem.

Attitudes—individuals' actions, behaviors, and points of view.

Community—distinct from an ecosystem, a community is a subset of the ecosystem. The startup community is made up of people who are spending 100 percent of their time on entrepreneurial endeavors.

Complex system—"systems whose behavior is intrinsically difficult to model due to the dependencies, competitions, relationships, or other types of interactions between their parts or between a given system and its environment."[37]

Complicated system—a system with many interacting parts—often created by man—that is well understood.[38]

Deal flow—the number of investment opportunities available to an investor. More quality opportunities are what great investors strive for.

Early stage—a period of time or maturity of the company's growth that ranges from idea to product rollout and revenue scaling.

Ecosystem—the ecosystem is broader than the community and includes actors that are one ring removed from the everyday activities of entrepreneurship. These typically include government, university, or corporate actors.

#givefirst—a concept by which you are willing to put energy into a relationship or a system without defining the transactional parameters. It isn't altruism, because you expect to get *something*. But you don't know when, from whom, in what form, or by what consideration.[39]

---

37 Wikipedia, s.v. "Complex System," last modified February 9, 2023, https://en.wikipedia.org/wiki/Complex_system.

38 Christoph von der Malsburg, July 31, 2012, comment on David Walker, "What is the difference between complex and complicated?," ResearchGate, July 31, 2012, https://www.researchgate.net/post/What-is-the-difference-between-complex-and-complicated.

39 Brad Feld and Ian Hathaway, *The Startup Community Way: Evolving an Entrepreneurial Ecosystem* (Hoboken: Wiley, 2020), 46–47.

System—a system has three basic elements: input, processing, and output. The other elements include control, feedback, boundaries, environment, and interfaces. Input is what data the system receives to produce a certain output. Processing is what happens when the data—and actions—are smashed together. What goes out from the system after being processed is known as Output.

Systems theory—a system is a cohesive conglomeration of interrelated and interdependent parts that can be natural or human-made. Every system is bounded by space and time, influenced by its environment, defined by its structure and purpose, and expressed through its functioning. A system may be more than the sum of its parts if it expresses synergy or emergent behavior.[40]

ORGANIZATIONS

Accelerator—a structured investment program that combines investment with fundamental mentorship over a fixed period of time (typically less than a year).

Chamber of Commerce—an organization that is responsible for helping businesses grow and prosper.

Coworking Space—offices, floors, or buildings made available to people of similar interests, jobs, personalities, etc. WeWork is an example.

Economic Development—groups and organizations that are

---

40 Wikipedia, s.v. "Systems Theory," last modified January 27, 2023, https://en.wikipedia.org/wiki/Systems_theory.

tasked with growing their economies in a specific geography (city, state, federal).

Incubator—an open-ended program that provides access to equipment, people, and space usually subsidized by the government or a university with no fixed time period and limited organized mentorship.

Startup—a company in the early stages of formation (idea to scaling product and staff).

PEOPLE

Angel investor—a person who writes a check for a financial instrument but invests as a person and not as an organized fund (see venture capitalist).

Entrepreneur—a person who is actively working on an idea for a company.

Founder—the person(s) who takes an initial idea and forms a company.

Influencer—someone whom others look to for advice, leadership, knowledge, etc. Former serial successful entrepreneurs are an example.

Investor—someone who provides money for some type of financial instrument (stock, note). I would add that if you have not written a check in over a year—you are not an investor.

Leader—someone who is typically assigned to a startup community role (Executive Director of the Entrepreneur Organization). A leader can also be a serial entrepreneur, an investor, or others who are actively involved.

Venture capitalist—a professional, full-time investor who has a dedicated investment fund.

MY STARTUP COMMUNITY THOUGHT LEADERS/ ORGANIZATIONS

Brad Feld—www.feld.com

Ian Hathaway—www.ianhathaway.org

Victor Hwang—www.victorh.co

Techstars—www.techstars.com

Kauffman Foundation—www.kauffman.org

Steve Case—www.revolution.com

Startup Champions Network—www.startupchampions.co

Anika Horn—www.anikahorn.com

FURTHER READING (BOOKS THAT INSPIRED ME)

Startup Communities: Building an Entrepreneurial Ecosystem in Your City—Brad Feld

The Startup Community Way: Evolving an Entrepreneurial Ecosystem—Brad Feld and Ian Hathaway

It's Not Complicated: The Art and Science of Complexity in Business—Rick Nason

Connected: The Surprising Power of Our Social Networks and How They Shape Our Lives—Nicholas A. Christakis and James H. Fowler

Systems Thinking for Social Change: A Practical Guide to Solving Complex Problems, Avoiding Unintended Consequences, and Achieving Lasting Results—David Peter Stroh

The Culture Code: The Secrets of Highly Successful Groups—Daniel Coyle

The Rainforest: The Secret to Building the Next Silicon Valley—Victor W. Hwang and Greg Horowitt

ACKNOWLEDGMENTS

I am enamored with the power of networks and the meaningful connections that come from being open to new perspectives, experiences, and cultures.

I want to thank Brad Feld and Ian Hathaway, who took time to do an early read of this book and of course changed everything for the better. Later draft help (a huge monster edit) came from Joe Queenan and Robbie Allen.

This book is built on the backs of the people who helped me develop its content. They include Larkin Garbee in Richmond, Virginia; Andres Benavides and Gonzalo Villaran in Lima, Peru; Andrew Greer and Jeff Keen in Kelowna, British Columbia; Crystal Vann Wallstrom, Dave Sanders, and Steve Franks in Fort Wayne, Indiana; Aaron Slodov, Ed Buchholz, and Bob Sopko in Cleveland, Ohio; Alex Gress in Buffalo, New York; Rich Fu and Yvie Tai in Taipei, Taiwan; Evans McMillion and Monique Adams in Norfolk, Virginia; and Jeff Ruble, Lee MacIlwinen, and Caroline Crowder in Columbia, South Carolina.

My first venture into understanding how to put this into practice came from an amazing team as we built this consulting practice inside Techstars. To David Cohen, David Brown, Nicole Glaros, and Max Kelly, who helped me shepherd this new business—thanks for understanding that this was a startup that became a real business. My amazing thought partner, Cali Harris, brought so much thought, structure, and perspective. Thanks, Cali—I truly miss our daily work together.

Other team members included Matt Helt, Oko Davaasuren, Kristina Rodriguez, Alex Krause Matlack, Clark Dever, Jack Greco, Rosa Cheng, and David Ling. You were all part of this journey, and your thoughts, insights, and experiences are buried throughout this book. In the Techstars orbit, I would like to thank Wendy Lea for the many discussions about what makes for a vibrant ecosystem. Wendy, we may not have engaged in activities like we always wanted, but I enjoyed our conversations and am richer for it. Pete Birkeland was an early book partner when we had the Techstars publishing team—Pete, thanks so much!

To the team at Scribe who helped me make this the best book it could be. Caroline Clouse, thanks for the effort to make me a better author.

Last, to the family who rides the roller coaster with me: Patty, Jessie, Wayne, Juliana, Ashley, Will, Ella, Henry, and Jacob.

ABOUT THE AUTHOR

CHRIS HEIVLY is probably the only geographer/entrepreneur that you might know. He has a bachelor's degree in geography from West Chester University and a master's degree in geography from the University of South Carolina. Most interestingly, Chris learned how to write code as an undergraduate geography student. He sometimes refers to himself as one of the first map geeks.

For over thirty years, Chris has worked at the highest levels at some of the world's most recognized brands, including MapQuest, which was later sold to AOL for $1.2 billion; Rand McNally, the world's largest map publisher; and Accenture, one of the largest multinational management consulting, technology services, and outsourcing companies on the planet. He has also personally directed over $75 million in investment capital on behalf of these and other companies.

Chris currently serves as one of two managing directors of The Startup Factory, one the largest seed investment firms in the Southeast. Under his leadership, the firm has made thirty-five investments in emerging-technology companies.

After TSF, Chris joined Techstars, the world's largest ecosystem that helps entrepreneurs build great businesses, to develop a new set of products and services focused on helping startup communities grow. This role leverages Chris's experience in building the Raleigh-Durham ecosystem with the expertise of Brad Feld (Foundry Group and Startup Communities) and the Techstars leadership. From 2017 to 2021, Heivly created a team of twelve, generated consulting engagements, and materially changed entrepreneurship in several underdeveloped cities.

Chris is a sought-after speaker and go-to source for the media. He has been quoted in major national and international outlets such as *Forbes, Inc.*, the *Washington Post, TechCrunch, Crain's Business Journal, Huffington Post, Tech Cocktail*, and the *Financial Times*, and has appeared on major-market TV stations across the US. He was featured in the documentary *Startupland*, which showcased the world's most renowned entrepreneurs and startup experts. Chris is a contributing writer for Inc.com, the nation's leading entrepreneurial magazine for entrepreneurs and business owners, and he has a significant following at www.heivly.com, his blog, which offers brutally authentic commentary on startups and startup community building.

His first book, *Build the Fort: Why 5 Simple Lessons You Learned as a 10-Year-Old Can Set You Up for Startup Success*, is about how to take the lessons you learned as a ten-year-old and apply them to starting anything. It was inspired by a widely acclaimed 2014 TEDx talk. The book focuses on the months leading up to the decision to start a company and those first three critical months of getting an idea off the ground. Its premises are being applied in multiple realms, from individuals with a dream, to startups and companies that aspire to be more innovative, to emerging entrepreneurial communities.

Today, Chris picks a handful of meaningful projects to get involved in that are focused on helping startup communities and their builders. In support of that mission he also produces and hosts a podcast, *Your Startup Community*, with Brad Feld and Ian Hathaway.

YOUR STARTUP COMMUNITY

Want to be part of my community? I want to be part of yours.

On my website, www.heivly.com, you'll find more information on how to effectively accelerate your community and ecosystem. I'm also able to connect you with other like-minded peers who may be able to help you move your community forward.

You can also reach out and connect with me via email: chris@ buildthefort.com.

Want to read more updates, or share your stories, experiments, wins, or challenges? Sign up and submit them on the www.heivly. com/community page and I'll post them for all to see.

Interested in diving deeper on any of these subjects? Brad, Ian, and I have an eight-part podcast called *Your Startup Community* available on all the major sites. Check it out on the Techstars website, www.techstars.com/the-line/podcasts/your-startup-community, or directly here: www.yourstartupcommunity.com.

We are looking for new guests—if interested, reach out and let me know.

My wife jokingly shares that Chris + microphone + audience = my happy place. I'm available globally for speaking engagements both in person and virtually. I bring a healthy dose of passion and humor, plus an engaging and enriching style to the stage, and my subject matter expertise is versatile. You won't be disappointed. If interested, send me a note at chris@buildthefort. com.